Truly Weird

Real-life Cases of the Paranormal

Jenny Randles

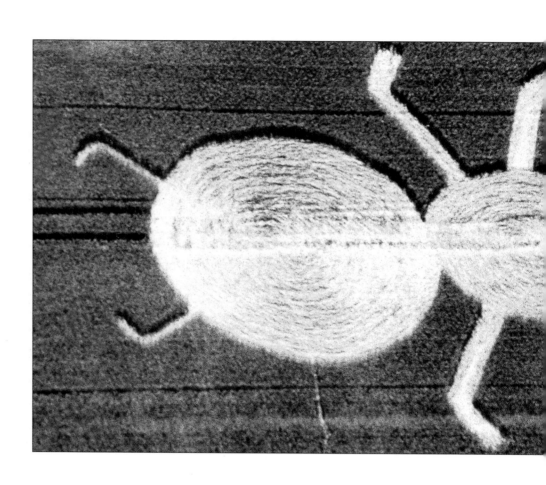

Jenny Randles

Truly Weird

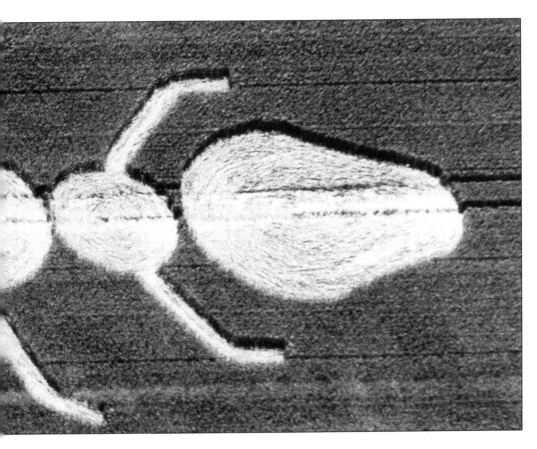

Real-life Cases
of the Paranormal

COLLINS & BROWN

First published in Great Britain in 1998 by
Collins & Brown Limited
London House
Great Eastern Wharf
Parkgate Road
London SW11 4NQ

1 3 5 7 9 8 6 4 2

British Library Cataloguing-in-Publication Data:
A catalogue record for this book
is available from the British Library.

ISBN 1 85585 442 2

Conceived, edited and designed by Collins & Brown Limited

Editorial Director: Sarah Hoggett
Art Director : Roger Bristow
Editor : Mary Lambert
Editorial Assistant: Simon Brockbank
Designers: Simon Ward-Hastelow, Claire Graham
Picture Researcher: Michael Nicholson

Reproduction by Colour Symphony, Singapore

Printed and bound in Italy

Contents

Introduction

THE STORY THAT follows is, like all the cases featured in this book, truly weird.

At 9 a.m. Peter Day was driving on a quiet country road near Cuddington from his Oxfordshire home to start work on designing the renovations needed on an old building. He took a movie camera with him so that he could film various aspects of the structure and study them at leisure. Suddenly, Peter saw a bright orange light low on the horizon to his north. As he drove alongside the light, he kept staring at it, wondering what it was. When he could stop, he did so, and took 23 seconds of film as the orange ball, pulsating in and out, moved silently behind some trees and then vanished.

Day continued his journey in a thoughtful mood. When he arrived back home later he discovered that an US Air Force F-111 jet from the nearby base at Upper Heyford had crashed in flames in a field near Milton Keynes, but the crew had ejected safely. Assuming that by chance he had filmed the last moments of the fated aircraft he called the base and offered the footage for use in their accident enquiry, but when he told them that he took the scenes at Cuddington at around 9.05 am the military lost interest: it turned out that the F-111 had crashed 35 minutes later, and miles away.

So what had Peter Day really witnessed? Was it a UFO? This is how the case came to my attention. I started to research it soon afterward and tried hard to work out what had happened. It was a long case and at times seemed hopeless, but ultimately we solved the mystery – at least to our satisfaction. Peter Day, however, remains unconvinced by the answer.

So what had happened to that orange ball over Cuddington? Was it really an alien craft? Perhaps. But years of research revealed other, less remarkable, explanations.

At the scene all the facts were gathered. The possible connection with the air crash was extensively probed. The plane was too remote from Cuddington at 9.05 am for the film to show the F-111 on fire. But the link between these two rare events – an air crash and a UFO sighting – was important. Unfortunately, we soon hit a problem: the files of this military incident were not actually released, as air accident enquiries usually are. Was this because there really had been a UFO which could have caused the disaster?

Meanwhile, the film analysis was proceeding. Study at the Kodak labs clearly told us that the footage was genuine. There was a large orange ball moving low across the horizon at maybe 322 kmph (200 mph), dependent upon distance and height. The weather data was also assessed. This showed a low cloud ceiling at about 610 metres (2000 ft). Whatever was visible could not be higher than that.

From this data a new idea developed. There is a rare weather effect known as 'ball lightning' that often forms as orange balls of light. This had never been filmed before, so scientists who studied it would be very excited if that was what Peter Day had recorded. So Kodak set aside their London offices and I spent a day screening the film and discussing the case with some leading atmospheric physicists.

Sadly, the scientists concluded that the film was not ball lightning. Each physicist was encouraged to take the film away for study. But they all refused. They stated they could not take the film because the stigma attached to investigating UFOs would count against them when they next applied for grant funding.

A Ministry of Defence military technologist agreed to study the film. He suggested that it might be a flashing orange light on top of a helicopter used as an experiment to aid visibility. However, these tests occurred months after the film was taken and not in this location.

Eventually, I persuaded the BBC to feature the case on a TV show we were making. Some witnesses were traced who had seen the ball at close quarters. After the programme I re-interviewed several of them and spoke to others who had not wanted to appear on national TV. This new evidence gave the impetus to the case that was needed.

Although uncertain about my conclusion I now had a reasonable idea of what might have happened and wrote a special publication, *Fire in the Sky*, that was published by BUFORA. Piecing together all the evidence and a new incident in which another F-111 jet got into trouble, even as I was writing the report, a scenario was proposed. The F-111 had developed a problem and tried to resolve it by venting ignited aviation fuel and letting it shoot from the rear of the plane like a flame thrower. This is only done in dire emergencies as it is risky. Fuel is dumped in case of an emergency landing where any spark could cause a fully laden fuel tank to explode. Given the weather conditions I suggested that the ejected fuel had formed a ball of fire that bounced along horizontally and was trapped by a thermal layer just above low cloud.

It was a guess. But it made sense of the evidence. Two years later it was seemingly vindicated when the USAF released details of their accident investigation into the F-111 crash. The crew had escaped using a then new rocket propulsion system developed from the Apollo space programme. This was secret and so the report had to remain so until the system was declassified.

From the file it was clear that the F-111 was indeed north of Cuddington at 9.05 am, flying in exactly the right direction. It had developed a fault on take-off and its crew had vented burning aviation fuel in preparation for an emergency landing. After a few minutes they abandoned this plan and flew in a giant circle for half an hour trying to use up fuel naturally, but the fault with the plane worsened and they had to eject before the jet crashed.

The orange ball of fire seen by witnesses and filmed by Peter Day could well have been this fuel, just as I had proposed. But this must remain a theory only: we can never totally prove that it was not a UFO.

Truly weird things like this happen every day. Welcome to the world of the 'supernaturalist' – someone who studies cases of the seemingly paranormal and tries to figure out what lies behind them.

Perhaps your only contact with such tales is through television programmes such as *The X-Files*, but what television never shows you is the sheer hard work that goes into resolving each mystery and the frustration that so often comes when you fail to identify the cause with any degree of certainty.

When you research the paranormal you are constantly faced with choices. On the one hand these are rational, perhaps credible and a little disappointing, but they are also extraordinary, hard to believe and earth-shattering. Striking a balance with each case is the true art of being a good supernaturalist. You should always seek a logical answer, expecting to find it and realizing it may well prove to be mundane. But in some cases incredible phenomena might well be taking place.

Each case is different. You never know which way it will go. Sometimes the answers will seem very down to earth. Sometimes all the evidence seems to turn scientific logic on its head. In many cases you will have to hedge your bets and decide which outcome best fits the known facts for this particular story.

But above all the quest to sift through a mysterious report and try to find out what caused the incident is unbelievably fascinating. This book will give you the chance to practise all those techniques and adopt a similar role to Mulder and Scully in *The X-Files* for a while.

Each chapter is a self-contained, real-life case. Many have been personally investigated and certainly I have researched all the phenomena in question. After the encounter is described by witnesses, many clues follow that will help in your quest to explain each case. Some of these are suggestions from witnesses; others are pieces of research conducted into each area by sceptics, believers or open-minded experts. There are also pointers to help you understand what might have taken place.

From then on it is down to you. Sort through the clues, assess the three options that I give for each case and decide which one you think provides the best explanation for the truly weird encounter. But if you want to know what I think I give my verdict for each at the end of the book, along with references to explore things further.

So search for the truth. It is out there somewhere – and it is your job to find it!

JENNY RANDLES

THE BERMUDA TRIANGLE ·THE BERMUDA TRIANGLE ·THE BERMUDA TRIANGLE ·THE BERMUDA TRI-
THE BERMUDA TRIANGLE ·THE BERMUDA TRIA·THE BERMU-
GLE ·THE BERMUDA TRIANGLE THE BERMU-
GLE ·THE BERMUDA TRIANGLE ·THE BERMUDA TRIANGLE ·THE BERMU-
·THE BERMUDA TRIANGLE ·THE BERMUDA TRIANGLE ·THE BERMUDA TRI-
ANGLE ·THE BERMUDA TRIANGLE ·THE BERMUDA TRIANGLE ·THE BERMU-

CASE STUDY

The Bermuda Triangle

The Flight to Nowhere

THE BERMUDA TRIANGLE: the legend that surrounds this ill-fated area of the Atlantic Ocean has persisted since 1945 with, according to some authorities, over 200 ships and aircraft disappearing within its boundaries. Air and sea rescue missions have found neither bodies nor wreckage. It is as if the unfortunate victims have somehow been sucked into oblivion – taken from this world by forces that lie far beyond our comprehension.

Over the years, many theories have been put forward to explain the strange disappearances in the Bermuda Triangle, but none have ever been conclusively proven. The testimony of men and women who have survived their terrifying experiences is our best – indeed, perhaps our only – chance of discovering the reasons behind the disappearances. In the investigation that follows, you will join one crew on its journey into one of the world's most feared areas and hear some of the theories put forward by expert witnesses to explain what really happened. Then you must try to decide for yourself.

As they flew out across the long stretch of open ocean leading towards Europe, things started to go terribly wrong.

Crisis on the Catalina

ONE SPRING DAY IN 1986, Martin Caidin, an experienced navigator and certainly not the sort of man who would be likely to invent wild stories, was on board a Catalina seaplane. It was heading from Florida for south-west England in order to carry out demonstration exercises and show off the flying skills of the machine. Because of the importance of the Catalina, Caidin and his team were equipped with multi-million-dollar safety devices. One such system included a sophisticated device that could receive signals from orbiting satellites and use them to plot the aircraft's position as it flew around the globe.

Everything was going smoothly as normal as the aircraft left Florida and crossed the South Atlantic towards the holiday island of Bermuda. But as they flew out across the long stretch of open ocean heading for Europe, things started to go terribly wrong. All of a sudden the navigation equipment went haywire. Computer displays spun wildly about. Everything appeared to be saturated in a vicious magnetic field. None of the instrumentation on board the aircraft was working and they had no means of knowing exactly where they were. With nothing but ocean surrounding them in all directions, this was a dangerous turn of events.

Caidin had only one thought: not again! Twenty-six years before he had been on board a US Air Force plane making the long haul from the eastern seaboard of the USA to the rocky isles of the Azores via Bermuda. There was little talk of the 'Triangle' back in 1960. It had yet to acquire its awesome reputation. They received a radio message advising them that radar showed their location as being about 80 minutes west of Bermuda. All was well.

Dead ahead, as the entire crew saw, Bermuda itself then loomed out of the ocean – plain as day. They called asking for confirmation of their position. It was verified. If they still had 80 minutes before they reached Bermuda, the island could not be visible – but there it was.

This was strange enough, but things were about to get a whole lot stranger. As the plane flew on, the image of the island grew no larger; despite their estimated speed of the 250 miles per hour, it was as if they were getting no nearer. None of the crew had ever experienced anything like this before. They repeatedly climbed up into cloud and descended again, trying to figure out what was happening, but the size of the island remained constant.

Just as suddenly, everything returned to normal. On their last descent from cloud, Bermuda appeared in sight and they flew towards it as Caidin had done so many times before. But on touchdown the ground staff were mystified. Where had the plane been? Why was it an hour late? The radar had shown them as being 80 minutes from landing,

A Catalina seaplane, similar to the one that took navigator Martin Caidin and his crew on their nightmare flight through the Bermuda Triangle.

but in fact they had taken two hours and twenty minutes to reach the island. The amount of fuel the aircraft had used up supported this.

Memories of that still unsolved riddle taxed Martin Caidin's mind as he concentrated on the controls of the Catalina in 1986. It was impossible to see the horizon. Wherever they looked, an impenetrable yellow mist met their gaze. Even the aircraft's own wingtips were invisible.

Caidin took the Catalina up and then down as far as he dared go without instrumentation. It made no difference; they were still engulfed in a murky, yellowish-gray soup, flying blind and hopelessly lost. If they were not heading towards land they could cruise on into thousands of miles of ocean until they ran out of fuel – and if that happened, then the one thing they could be sure of was that they had little chance of survival.

The only thing Caidin could do was steer the Catalina towards the lightest patch of yellow mist in the hope that this would provide an escape route. The crew made desperate calls for assistance but only the hiss of static filled the airwaves. If anybody could hear them, then nobody was answering their appeals for help.

They estimated the nightmare continued for about four hours. By now the small crew on the Catalina were fighting

despair. Soon they would start to run out of options. Then, just as dramatically as it had begun, their nightmare ended. Suddenly the aircraft plunged into clear blue sky and the strange yellow mist was nowhere to be seen.

Caidin tried all the instruments. Everything seemed to be working properly and the navigation system was now able to plot and show their position. They were back on course. However, the radio revealed that they had been flying for only one hour – not the four hours they had estimated. It was as if the aircraft had been temporarily taken out of normal time and had entered another dimension.

Only later did the realization dawn on the crew that they had been flying through the so-called Bermuda Triangle. To his amazement, Martin Caidin collected reports from other pilots and from ships who had similar stories to tell about other accidents over the years. He even learnt from a secret source at NASA that some orbiting space missions suffered mysterious communications blackouts whenever they happened to pass over this area of the Atlantic Ocean.

So what really happened to the ships and planes caught in the Bermuda Triangle? Is there any logical explanation for the strange disappearances, mysterious fogs and subsequent instrument malfunction? Let us take a look at some of the theories.

> *The radio revealed that they had been flying for only one hour – not the four hours they had estimated.*

The Bermuda Triangle

Modern Myth: The Cynic's View

AMERICAN FOLKLORE RESEARCHER Loren Coleman has made a study of locations that have attracted more than their fair share of supernatural stories down through the centuries. He notes that many of them have a name that links them with demonic activity. This simply denotes the superstitious way in which our ancestors interpreted events that could not be explained in any other way.

According to some researchers, the idea of the Bermuda triangle is nothing more than a modern myth. The most notable sceptic is Larry Kusche who, in 1975, wrote *The Bermuda Triangle Mystery Solved*.

> *The accidents seem incredible only if they are taken out of context of all the thousands of flights and ship passages that suffer no mishap whatsoever.*

Kusche traced the original accident reports of many cases in which ships or aircraft were said to have vanished without trace. Often he discovered that the writers had omitted to mention that wreckage was later found, or that the ship was carrying explosive cargo, or that there was a terrible storm raging at the time – any of which could be a factor that that could rationally explain a disappearance. Kusche also points out that the triangle falls within one of the most densely trafficked shipping and air routes in the world. Because of the numbers of craft traversing this zone every day, sheer statistics argue that more of them will get into trouble and suffer tragic accidents. The accidents seem incredible only if they are taken out of context of all the thousands of flights and ship passages that suffer no mishap whatsoever.

Because of the area's reputation, however, many people are only too ready to ascribe any accident to a

---

FLIGHT 19

ONE OF THE most significant incidents involving the Bermuda Triangle happened in 1945, with the disappearance of Flight 19 – a military training group of five Grumman Avenger torpedo bombers carrying 14 men. All the crew members, apart from their instructor, Lieutenant Charles Taylor, were trainees with limited experience. However, even Lieutenant Taylor was new to the area and had not flown this particular training exercise before.

At 2.10pm on 5 December 1945 the formation left Fort Lauderdale in Florida on, ironically, a triangular route – east towards the Bahamas, then north, and finally back to base. Each aircraft carried enough fuel to cruise for over 1000 miles and the flight time was calculated at two hours.

About an hour into the mission the previously fine weather deteriorated badly. The aircraft were soon flying in poor conditions, in the dark over an area that none of the crew (including their teacher) knew well.

At 3.40pm another aircraft landing at Fort Lauderdale reported hearing a radio conversation between two of the aircraft on Flight 19. Charles Taylor was apparently disputing with his senior trainee as to whether they had made a wrong turn. Taylor thought they were due south of Miami in the Florida Keys; an area he knew well, which is similar to the Cays near the Bahamas, where they were headed. Taylor also reported that he had problems with navigational instruments and could not get a compass bearing.

It seems that Taylor commanded the flight to head north. If they really had been south of Miami, they supernatural cause – making the area a modern-day 'devil zone'. An example of how facts can be distorted can be seen in the story of the disappearance of the Japanese freighter, the *Raifuku Maru*, in 1952. Somehow word has gotten around that the last message received from the freighter was a hysterical cry of 'Danger like dagger – come quick!' In fact the enquiry into the vessel's disappearance found that the message was in fact severely distorted by an electrical storm and that the last words uttered before the ship sank are more likely to have been a plea in broken English of 'Now very dangerous – come quick!'

Freak Storms: The Meteorologist's Theory

FREAK WEATHER CONDITIONS seem to be a recurring feature of many Bermuda Triangle stories. We have already heard about the strange yellow mist reported by Martin Caidin and the crew of the Catalina. Amongst the many other reports of strange activity in the Triangle, one case recorded by the American press in July 1904 seems particularly relevant to this aspect of Bermuda investigations.

It occurred at a time of severe electrical storms on the eastern seaboard of the USA, some of which featured peculiar 'balls of light' in the sky.

The *Mohican*, a medium-sized cargo ship with a crew of about a dozen, was heading out from Delaware into the Atlantic when the crew found themselves sailing into a gray and yellow cloud which seemed to be filled with a strange crackling energy. Each one of the ship's instruments was magnetized in such a way that they stuck to one another. The members of the crew were charged with what appeared to be static electricity and their hair and beards stood on end like stiff wire brushes. The *Mohican* sailed on, leaving this localized cloud and returning to normality, and none of those on board ever experienced anything like that again.

Clearly the events experienced by the crew members of the *Mohican* were due to some rare and, as yet, unexplained natural phenomenon associated with the electrical storms in the area. Perhaps it is an event that rarely happens in this region and which is the cause of the complete disorientation and loss of communications that are sometimes reported by ships and aircraft coming through the Bermuda Triangle.

> *The members of the crew were charged with what appeared to be static electricity, their hair and beards stood on end*

---

would have soon found land. If, as the trainee thought, they were east of Florida, turning due north would have taken them over thousands of miles of open ocean – a manoeuvre for which they did not have enough fuel.

Radio communications were bad due to the weather and the fact that Flight 19 was probably now far off course. Scattered reception, did on two occasions, pick up students trying to persuade Taylor to head west. The last message heard was the suggestion that, as they were now lost and running out of fuel, all the planes should ditch together when the first plane was forced to do so. If they had decided to abandon their planes in the rough Atlantic they would not have been able to survive for very long.

Several rescue planes were sent up at this point. One of these – a Mariner, with 13 men on board –

vanished suddenly without sending an SOS. The others returned safely. A passing ship reported seeing a mid-air explosion and wreckage falling into the sea. It seems likely the Mariner blew up for some reason; there had been similar problems with this type of aircraft in previous bad weather.

According to some reports of Flight 19, radio messages from the crew – none of which have been verified – reported that the sea looked 'strange' and warned others not to come after them. This does not form part of the official record and no confirmed witnesses have ever come forward to support the claim. Despite an extensive air and sea search over several days, no wreckage, oil slicks or bodies from the ill-fated Flight 19 were ever found, and the mystery has never been solved.

Windows On Another World: The Paranormal Investigator's Theory

THE WAY IN WHICH the *Catalina* seaplane seemed to disappear into another reality where time and space had different rules is typical of many cases reported from within the Bermuda Triangle. Does this imply that a doorway exists between our reality and another?

The idea that there are windows in which strange phenomena can intrude into our reality was first suggested by New York journalist, John Keel. He had investigated numerous reports of monsters and strange aliens that seemed to defy logic. He came to believe that all sorts of supernatural entities can flow through into our world from other dimensions by way of 'windows' at spots where the boundary between one world and another is very weak.

Research into the seemingly infinite nature of the cosmos was given a boost by the theories of relativity defined by Albert Einstein in the early years of the twentieth century. In essence, Einstein argued that the speed of light represents not a barrier but a transition between realities. Experiments with fast-moving sub-atomic particles have now proved Einstein's amazing ideas. Equations show that, once the speed of light is exceeded, a kind of mirror universe must exist in which the laws of nature are opposite to those in our own world. To reach this place without travelling at the speed of light requires passage through an interdimensional window, known to physicists as a 'wormhole'. We have yet to prove the existence of these naturally occurring links through time and space, but astronomers increasingly believe they exist – possibly in connection with black holes. Black holes are areas of the universe where time and space are so distorted by massive gravity fields that light itself cannot escape. If something enters a black hole, it may vanish from the reality of everything else within our universe. This is chillingly similar to the way in which ships and aircraft – such as Flight 19 – vanish from areas like the Bermuda Triangle.

Physicists believe that that a wormhole is like a tunnel that punctures the everyday flow of time and space. It acts as a short-cut between two completely different parts of the cosmos. For example, if you fall down one end of a tunnel, you may think you have taken only a few moments to reach the other end and have moved a relatively short distance. However you may emerge on the other side in a completely different part of the universe – perhaps many light years from where you started.

The statements of witnesses such as Martin Caidin and James McGregor could possibly indicate the existence of portals through which people and things occasionally slip at random.

*Scientifiction
Stories by*

A. Hyatt Verrill
John W. Campbell, Jr.
Edmond Hamilton

A. Hyatt Verrill's tale 'The Non-gravitational Vortex' prefigured the acceleration of the Bermuda Triangle mystery by twenty years.

Magnetic Fields: The Geologists' Theory

DETAILED RESEARCH CONDUCTED by geologists during the 1970s and 1980s has uncovered a number of important clues about the nature of the earth as a dynamic body floating in space. These discoveries may explain why the ill-fated crew of Flight 19 and navigator Martin Caidin aboard his Catalina seaplane experienced such bizarre interference to their sophisticated communications systems.

Geophysicists have discovered that a very strong magnetic field is generated by the liquid metal that circulates deep inside the Earth's core. However, it was not until recently that we began to understand exactly just how much this magnetic field might affect events taking place on the Earth's surface.

Experiments performed by geologist Dr Brian Brady at the US Bureau of Mines in Boulder, Colorado, demonstrated that electrical energy is released by rocks with a high crystalline content, producing light effects within the atmosphere. British geologist Dr Paul McCartney took Brady's experiments one stage further by placing large pieces of rock under pressure in laboratory conditions, using high-speed cameras to record what happened before the force caused the rock to shatter. Short-lived gleams of light were produced which floated close to the rock's surface. These mysterious glows appear to be caused by electrical energy released from the rock triggering reactions in the gases of the atmosphere.

Paul Devereux, a professional 'earth mysteries' researcher who seeks to explain the pattern of relationships between human beings and the landscape throughout the centuries, has researched strange phenomena and believes that they often have a rational explanation. He worked with McCartney on the project and coined the term 'earthlights' for these glowing lights. He suspected that on a larger scale outside the laboratory the lights would be much bigger and longer-lasting and would float freely above the surface of the Earth, riding on the magnetic currents that the planet naturally generates.

These earthlights have their own associated magnetic fields, since magnetism is created by moving electricity. It was speculated that if someone were to drive close by one of these hovering lights the resulting electrical effects might well distort the operating system of the vehicle. There are many attested cases of car engines and lights failing in the presence of what the witnesses claim to be UFOs – although in truth it is likely that these UFOs are nothing more than glowing balls of electrical energy.

Although Devereux's interest lies primarily in the examination of UFOs, his research is nonetheless relevant to studies of the Bermuda Triangle. Earthlights are likely to concentrate in locations where geological and magnetic fields are strongest – areas that we might otherwise, adopting the terminology invented by paranormal investigator John Keel, refer to as 'window areas'.

If one of these zones really were to exist in the Atlantic Ocean near Bermuda, might it offer some explanation as to why ships and aircraft passing through the area sometimes record magnetic and electrical interference?

There are many attested cases of car engines and lights failing in the presence of what the witnesses claim to be UFOs.

Transients: The Neurophysiologist's Theory

IN 1977, CANADIAN neuro-physiologist Dr Michael Persinger published the results of a study with Ghyslaine Lafreniere into thousands of reports of strange phenomena in North America, ranging from UFOs to ghosts. Persinger and Lafreniere were trying to find a geographical pattern. Find one they did: there was a link with magnetic fields.

Persinger correlated hotspots of paranormal activity with the Earth's magnetic fields and fault lines occurring naturally in rocks below the surface. From this he postulated the existence of what he called 'transients' – pockets of electromagnetic energy created by the magnetic forces inside the earth and localized within what John Keel calls 'window areas'.

Persinger believed that these transients might produce earthlights and, moreover, anyone who encounters a transient might well become aware of its presence in other more subtle ways: the electrical energy would cause the person's hair to stand up on end and their skin to tingle. This is exactly the type of physiological effect that witnesses have often described as experiencing at the onset of strange phenomena. Persinger designed a machine that could create an

Grumman Avenger aircraft similar to those that flew on the ill-fated sortie over the Triangle.

artificial electro-magnetic transient in the laboratory and exposed people to it in differing intensities. Mild exposure to the energy field resulted in spatial disorientation – or a sense of 'unreality' – as well as the first stages of an altered state of consciousness. This is another feature reported by witnesses at the beginning of a paranormal encounter.

At higher levels of intensity, some of Persinger's subjects experienced various hallucinations – lights and ghostly shapes which appear to be unearthly in origin. Persinger also reported that transients can distort spacial and temporal awareness.

Michael Persinger now suggests that many types of paranormal event occur when natural energy transients form in the atmosphere above a magnetized fault zone. When a witness comes into contact with the transient, he or she may be led into a series of 'out of this world' hallucinations.

Persinger's theory means that if a ship or aircraft were to pass through a large drifting transient, the electromagnetic effects might result in the people on board experiencing distortions to time and space. Repeatedly we hear of witnesses claiming that, while they were undergoing their strange experiences in the Bermuda Triangle, time appeared to flow 'differently' than normal.

Missing In Action

O VER THE YEARS, MANY SHIPS and aircraft have disappeared in curious circumstances whilst traversing the so-called Bermuda Triangle. But few could be so tragic, or potentially catastrophic, as the loss of the USS *Scorpion* – a nuclear submarine with a crew of 99. The story of her final voyage is a good example of how evidence about this mysterious region can be misinterpreted.

The *Scorpion* had taken part in naval exercises off the coast of Italy and then set sail for its home base in Norfolk, Virginia. Just before midnight on 21 May 1968, she surfaced to make a routine call to state that she was heading west across the Atlantic and would reach home within the week. She never got there.

At first, there was no panic. There were storms off the eastern seaboard and it was assumed that the *Scorpion* was riding these out. But then, on the evening of 29 May, several naval vessels south-east of Virginia picked up a curious message. It was a routine transmission relaying the code for the *Scorpion*, along with a standard request for receipt of the message. Coupled with the fact that the submarine was two days overdue, a search was initiated, but nothing was found at the point of transmission by the ships and aircraft involved.

On 28 October a US naval survey ship, the *Mizar*, found the *Scorpion*. It was 10,000 feet below the waves, at a point between the Azores and Bermuda. Its hull had been crushed like an eggshell after it had submerged too deep, and fallen victim to the huge pressure that exists at such a depth. Thankfully, no nuclear detonation had occurred, but extensive investigation failed to reveal any cause for the disaster. Underwater examination of the wreck showed no sign of attack, on-board explosion or indeed any evident malfunction. Something had caused the vessel to sink too deep – and so fast – that the crew could do nothing to escape their fate. It seemed as if the Bermuda Triangle had claimed one of its most dangerous victims.

But what of the message that had been detected? There was a huge problem regarding this. In fact, the US Navy branded it a hoax very quickly. Yet the correct code name had been transmitted on a true frequency used by submarines – so how?

There was good reason why the US Navy felt the message could not really be from the *Scorpion*. Although they had kept it secret until just before the wreck was discovered, they knew the vessel had been destroyed – and that the crew were dead – several days before the message was

picked up. By chance an underwater sound recording team had taped the last frantic moments of the *Scorpion* as it reported 'We are breaking up all around' – followed by the sickening noise of the submarine imploding. By the time the 'sound echo' message was received, the US Navy was already searching for the wreck of the vessel.

The details of the disturbing end of the *Scorpion* were not released for several reasons. As the search was under-way already, the authorities saw no need to draw attention to the fact the sub was already destroyed. They also saw no need to cause widespread panic at the potentially devastating consequences created by the destruction of a vessel with nuclear capabilities. So, to avoid concern and government 'embarrassment', the search quietly continued, the US Navy, keen to find the wreck to verify its nuclear payload, had not been compromised.

As such, the message cannot presumably have any connection to the tragedy. It might have been a hoax by a radio amateur aware of the missing vessel and familiar with emergency frequencies. Or by coincidence it could have referred to a ship with a real name that matched the code name of the *Scorpion*'s last recorded mission – 'Brandywine'. It is possible that ships of the same name could have sent the message.

But what caused the death of the submarine? Possibly just a malfunction. Five years later, the USS *Greenling* almost suffered a similar fate, narrowly avoiding being crushed after submerging too far due to a faulty depth monitor. So perhaps it was just another tragic accident after all.

So What Did Happen?

You now have the facts to make up your own mind about what happened. Here are some possibilities.

● *The Bermuda Triangle is simply a myth. Quite mundane circumstances blocked the communications systems. Adverse weather conditions, such as unusually thick cloud, compounded the problem. Because of the area's reputation, things that, in other circumstances, would not be considered unusual were interpreted as something far more sinister.*

● *Window areas exist within the Earth's electro-magnetic field which can become unbalanced to*

form a 'transient' - one of which the Catalina flew through on that day. Severe electrical disturbances resulted, blocking out all communications. It affected the witnesses by triggering hallucinations that made them perceive time and space differently. A genuine energy cloud may also have been present, making it appear as if the aircraft could not escape the strange mist that surrounded it.

● *Wormholes act like tunnels between different parts of the cosmos. One of these temporarily formed in the local time-space framework above the Atlantic as the Catalina flew on its course, acting as a doorway into another dimension.*

SPONTANEOUS HUMAN COMBUSTION · SPONTANEOUS HUMAN COMBUS-
TION · SPONTANEOUS HUMAN COMBUSTION · SPONTANEOUS HUMAN
COMBUSTION · SPONTANEOUS HUMAN COMBUSTION · SPONTA-
NEOUS HUMAN COMBUSTION · SPONTANEOUS HUMAN COMBUSTION
SPONTANEOUS HUMAN COMBUSTION · SPONTANEOUS HUMAN
TION · SPONTANEOUS HUMAN COMBUSTION · SPONTANEOUS HUMAN

CASE STUDY

Spontaneous Human Combustion

The Case of The Cinder Woman

MARY HARDY REESER'S DEATH was both shocking and bizarre, and one which baffled not only the police but also the FBI. It was also to become known as a landmark case in the study of the terrifying phenomenon known as spontaneous human combustion. We know that Mary Reeser, recently widowed, had moved from her beloved home in Columbia, Pennsylvania to be nearer her son, Dr Richard Reeser, and his family in St Petersburg, Florida. We know, too, that she was very homesick and was planning to move back to her home town. She hated Florida's hot and sticky climate and was generally unsettled and depressed. Did these factors have any influence on why or how she died? From the evidence, you can decide whether Mary Reeser's death really was a case of the ancient and mysterious phenomenon of the 'fire from nowhere'.

A Routine Day

ON SUNDAY 1 JULY 1951, Mary followed her usual routine. She rose at 6am and listened to the radio. Her neighbour and landlord, Pansy Carpenter, heard its tones waft through the air and then heard Mary do some washing. Eventually the sprightly 67-year-old went into town to run some errands for her son Richard, before walking to his house to join his wife and their three children for dinner.

Mary arrived a little early that Sunday and offered to look after her youngest grandchild whilst Richard and his wife Ernestine took their other daughters to the beach. Richard could see that Mary was depressed and after an hour he returned to find her sobbing in an armchair.

She explained that a friend of hers was supposed to collect her this weekend so that they could go back to Pennsylvania and look for somewhere for Mary to live. Sadly, that friend had broken her leg, therefore making the trip impossible. Mary was in despair.

Mary Hardy Reeser. Key questions on the circumstances surrounding her death remain unanswered.

Abandoning the evening meal she asked Richard to take her home, but he was dirty from the beach and needed a shower first. Mary decided not to wait for him and had already set off walking back on her own before Richard was ready to drive her home. Ernestine set off to try to catch up with her mother-in-law but Mary Reeser had already reached her apartment block on Cherry Street by then. It was now 5pm.

Richard Reeser was becoming increasingly concerned about his mother's state of mind, so at 8pm he drove around to Mary's apartment on Cherry Street with one of his daughters. To their relief, they found the elderly woman now much more relaxed. She had taken two Seconal sleeping tablets and was wearing a nightdress with a fan set up to cool her down as she sat in her well-stuffed easy chair. They chatted for a while and then, reassured that his mother was now feeling much more positive, Richard Reeser and his daughter drove home.

A Hint of Danger

AFTER THE REESERS HAD LEFT, Pansy Carpenter came in from next door for a chat. Mary was wearing slippers and still not in bed. She was disappointed at not being able to go on the house-hunting trip but otherwise seemed well. After about half an hour Pansy went to buy some ice cream, but on her return just before 9pm, she noticed that the lights were off and the radio silent. Assuming that Mrs Reeser had gone to bed she decided not to disturb her. Nobody else was to see Mary Reeser alive again.

At 5am on the Monday, Pansy Carpenter was woken by a dull thudding noise. She went outside to investigate but saw nothing strange although she could smell what appeared to be the faint odour of electrical burning. Fearing a possible short circuit she turned off a water pump in the garage as a precaution and returned to bed, unable to find any obvious source for the smell and dismissing it as her imagination. Around 6.30am she collected the newspaper delivered by young Bill Connor who had seen, heard and smelt nothing strange as he approached the Allamanda Apartments where Mary lived.

Pansy was disturbed again at about 8am by a Western Union telegram delivery boy called Richard Bruce. He had news for Mary Reeser and asked to be directed to her apartment. Pansy explained that she had to take the newspaper over to let Mary read it and so would drop off the telegram as well. This message had brought Mary the glad tidings that a promising new property had just come onto the market in Columbia, where she wished to return.

Sadly Mary was never to read that welcome news, and Pansy Carpenter was soon about to make the most terrifying and disturbing discovery of her life.

A Terrifying Discovery

AS MRS CARPENTER ARRIVED at Mary's three-room suite she noticed the screen door was ajar and the handle of the door was very hot. Fearing the worst, Pansy yelled out to the telegram boy, but Richard Bruce continued on his route down Cherry Street. Then she screamed more loudly at some decorators working across the road and within moments these men, followed by Bruce, scurried over to the apartment block.

One man entered and urged Pansy Carpenter to call the fire brigade. She did so and also rang Dr Richard Reeser. When they entered the apartment, they discovered that just one wooden joist was on fire – easily extinguished with a hand pump. Assistant Fire Chief Griffiths then opened the windows to let the smoke clear but noticed there was minimal damage to the room. However, their relief was to be short-lived.

Pansy Carpenter was soon about to make the most terrifying and disturbing discovery of her life.

Only then did the fire crew realize that Mary Reeser was still in the building – or rather, what was left of her. Just one foot protruded from a pile of ashes that lay scattered on the ground like a raked out fire grate.

Yet in spite of the fact that Mary Reeser's body had been reduced to a pile of ashes with almost no recognizable features remaining, the area that immediately surrounded her body was relatively unscathed. Simply the one foot – eerily untouched – stuck out from the shocking debris that had once been a human being.

How can this possibly have happened? What caused a fire devastating enough to disintegrate a human body to leave the surrounding area more or less untouched? What sort of fire failed to melt nearby plastic, scorch wood only inches from the body of Mary Reeser or even touch highly flammable paper on the adjacent table?

Spontaneous Human Combustion

Mary Spontaneously Combusted!: The Media's Conclusion

THE LOCAL PRESS WERE QUICK to seize on the details of this mysterious case and label the unfortunate Mary as 'The Cinder Woman'. Of course, graphic sensationalist headlines like this are great for selling newspapers – but is there any reason to suspect that Mary really did spontaneously burst into flames? The following two reports from survivors may shed some light on Mary's case – although, in the absence of any eyewitness account of Mary's tragic death, we may never know the full story.

Medical doctor John Overton reported one of the earliest cases in the *Transactions of the Medical Society of Tennessee*. He reports the trauma suffered by Professor James Hamilton, a mathematics lecturer at the University of Nashville, on 5 January 1835. While checking a weather recording instrument in his garden on that cold winter's day the professor reported that he suddenly felt 'a steady pain like a hornet's sting, accompanied by a sensation of heat ... Looking at my left leg I distinctly saw light flame of the extent of a ten-cent piece having a complexion which nearest resembles that of pure quicksilver.'

After several attempts to slap out the flames, the professor decided to try to cut off the oxygen supply. He cupped his hands around the flames, which leapt several inches from his body. The searing pain lessened in extent and the fire disappeared completely. Once indoors he investigated and found serious burns, which took several days to heal and left a scar. These appeared to emanate from deep within his leg. There was a burn mark in his underpants but his trousers were not burnt, simply yellowed at the immediate point of contact. The flame had originated within the body and had burnt its way outwards.

Perhaps it was only the professor's knowledge of science that allowed him to escape being completely consumed by this deadly fire. He realized that without oxygen the flames could not survive. Other more instinctive methods (such as trying to beat out the fire) are more likely to be attempted by non-specialists and these seem to have no effect.

Another survivor was Paul Castle who claimed to have sprouted flames as he walked along the high

The phenomenon of the 'fire from nowhere' has been recorded throughout history.

street in Stepney Green, London, on 25 May 1985. He later described what happened: 'It sounded like a huge gas flame being lit. I could feel the flames burning, as if I'd been doused in petrol and set on fire.'

Paul collapsed onto the floor and rolled into a ball, in the very same way that Professor Hamilton had done 150 years earlier, attempting to put out the flames by stifling the oxygen supply.

He survived, noting afterwards: 'I gingerly felt my face, hair, arms, neck and chest. I was numb in some spots. White in others. I staggered through the doors of the local emergency room and was treated for my burns. They were extensive but superficial.'

No evidence was found that he had been set on fire by any normal means. He was not a smoker. No accelerants – such as petrol – were found on his clothing. He was another lucky survivor of the mysterious force known as spontaneous human combustion.

Accidental Death: The Doctor's Diagnosis

D R RICHARD REESER strongly supports the opinion that there is no supernatural mystery behind his mother's tragic demise in 1951. In 1991, then in his eighties, he reported in a letter: 'My mother was an overweight woman of five foot, accustomed to taking a night-time sedative, in this case Seconal, and she was a cigarette smoker.

'After visiting her around 9pm she was dressed in her nightie sitting in a large overstuffed chair with two fans blowing. Her turned-down bed was about three feet away. She had taken two Seconal tablets and she was smoking. In my opinion (my wife concurs) she fell asleep in the chair, the cigarette fell into the corner of the chair and began smouldering.

CORONER KEEPS AN OPEN MIND

A T 10.30AM ON 28 DECEMBER 1987, Detective Sergeant Nigel Cruttenden of the Kent CID was called to a flat attached to a bakery in Folkestone. On the floor in the kitchen by the cooker were the very badly incinerated remains of a man. The only things that were left of him were his feet and training shoes. Cruttenden took notes that plastic utensils were only inches away and yet were untouched by the fire. Polystyrene tiles on the ceiling were also not affected in any way. After eliminating the idea that the victim – 44-year-old Barry Soudain – had been murdered elsewhere and dumped in the kitchen, the police focused their attention on the lit cooker ring near the body. The forensic team were left with only one possible answer – that Soudain had fallen onto the lit ring, caught alight and died as a result – slowly combusting through the wick effect (see p.22). The gap between the last time he was seen alive and the discovery of the body was sufficiently long – some 15 hours – for this to be a possibility.

Coroner Brian Smith reported that the possibility of spontaneous human combustion in this case left him with an open mind, as there were many questions that remained unanswered. So much of the body was destroyed by the extraordinary localized fire that investigation was difficult. However, one thing that contradicts the wick effect theory is the fact that in this case we can be quite certain that the body cannot have been burning for anything like as long as 15 hours.

We know this because the first person to enter the room and find the body was Soudain's landlord. He reported that he had found a kettle half filled with water, partly resting on the lit cooker ring. As there was no sign of a forced entry and the only victim was in the flat that night, he must have placed the kettle on that cooker himself. Basic physics dictates that the water in it would have boiled away – and burnt a hole through the base of the kettle – long before sufficient time had elapsed to allow the wick effect to operate.

Although we therefore know that Barry Soudain died no more than an hour or so before his remains were discovered, we are no closer to finding the cause of his death.

'The draft created by the fans produced a steady furnace-like fire that ultimately consumed everything. A few chair springs were found beside the skull plate and heel bone of my mother. That's it. That's the way it was. Of course, an unusual, to say the least, and spectacular death, with quite an astonishing end.'

Dr Reeser's theory has the backing by Jo Nickell and John Fisher, who have studied the death of Mary Reeser for articles in the *Fire and Arson Investigator* and *Skeptical Enquirer* – the latter published by the anti-paranormal organisation CSICOP (Committee for the Scientific Investigation of Claims of the

When she was found soon after 8am the next morning, the bones in her body were discovered to have been 'cooked' as if in an oven, thus turning to ash.

Paranormal). The men are well qualified; Fisher has worked as an analyst at a Florida crime lab and Nickell was a private detective.

Nickell and Fisher argue that Mrs Reeser accidentally caught alight soon after 9pm on the Sunday. Being heavily sedated, she failed to wake up and was overcome by smoke and then slowly combusted over the course of the next 11 hours. When she was found soon after 8am the next morning, the bones in her body were discovered to have been 'cooked' as if in an oven, thus turning to ash. In evidence Nickell and Fisher note that certain statements

Ranchers inspect the wreckage from the skies on William Brazel's land, Roswell, in 1947.

There were simply pieces of foil and wood everywhere in the gully.

It was while out shopping in the small town of Corona that Brazel first heard about the mystery of the 'flying saucers'. Being rather cut off in his remote ranch in the days before TV, he had missed the furore that began about 10 days earlier, when a pilot called Kenneth Arnold had reported seeing a strange object over the Cascade Mountains in Washington State. It was the start of a new era and the press had dubbed these things 'flying discs' or 'flying saucers'. By now the nation was intrigued. One media source had offered $5000, a large sum of money in those days, for exclusive proof of the craft.

Now convinced he might really have captured something valuable, Brazel drove into Roswell on Sunday 6 July and told Sheriff George Wilcox that he had pieces of what he thought might be a flying saucer that had crashed on his ranch. When he ascertained that Brazel was not joking, the sheriff inspected the debris in the back of the pick-up and ordered his two deputies to go out to the Foster ranch and inspect the crash site. He also told the rancher that he thought they should inform the Roswell base.

This base was a major player in town politics, as it was the only squadron in the world equipped to fly the atom bomb. These devices were built 200 miles away at Los Alamos, in the north of New Mexico, and test explosions occurred near Alamogordo, about 100 miles west of Roswell. Other sensitive research into rocket technology that preceded America's first space flight was also occurring nearby at White Sands Proving Grounds. Wilcox clearly knew that any strange object found in these parts was important enough to share with the authorities.

By chance, as they were talking this over a local radio reporter called them to ask for the latest news of any arrests. In such a small town these rarely amounted to much and normally just included the odd ranch hand who had drunk too much. So the reporter was amazed to be told that a local rancher had just walked in with pieces of what seemed to be a crashed flying saucer. However, rather strangely, the reporter decided to await for advice from the base before reporting on what could possibly have become a legendary exclusive.

After lunch, intelligence officer Major Jesse Marcel arrived at the sheriff's office from the Roswell base. He was obviously in no great hurry, but had come out to look into the matter. He was clearly impressed with the material shown to him by Mac Brazel and George Wilcox. He told the sheriff to look after the rancher and took some debris back to the base for further study. Here he sought some advice from his commanding officer, Colonel

> *Other sensitive research into rocket technology that preceded America's first space flight was also occurring nearby at White Sands Proving Grounds.*

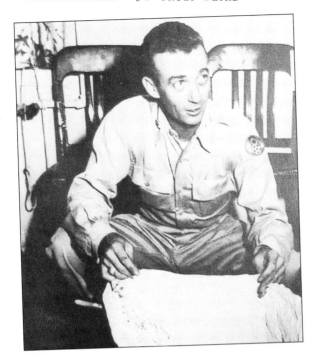

The U-turn: Major Jesse Marcel displays the balloon debris the military claim was from Roswell.

William Blanchard, who suggested that Marcel take a senior counter-intelligence officer with him and go out to the ranch. They were aware that the wreckage might be a foreign spy device.

Marcel chose to take Captain Sheridan Cavitt with him and the two men went back to the sheriff's to meet Brazel. Meanwhile, Colonel Blanchard called his commander, General Roger Ramey, at the Carswell base in Fort Worth, Texas. Washington DC was then immediately informed of the findings after this consultation.

Marcel, Cavitt and Brazel set off for the Foster Ranch that afternoon in a convoy of three vehicles. It was a long drive and the men decided not to work in the dark, but instead planned to make an early start on the Monday morning. In the meantime the two deputies sent by Sheriff Wilcox to the ranch had returned saying that they were unable to find the wreckage without Brazel's help, but also stated that they had seen an area of burnt ground.

Back at the base in Roswell orders had come through to Blanchard from Colonel Thomas DuBose at Carswell.

> *The rancher was placed under house arrest for a week. Cavitt took several military police with him and roadblocks were set up to secure the crash site.*

These were sent direct from the Pentagon, he advised, and stated that a sample of wreckage should be sent to Texas and then flown on to Wright Field in Dayton, Ohio.

The US Air Force's Foreign Technology Division (FTD) was at the Wright Patterson Air Force base, as it is now known. Its job was to collect material from any wrecked foreign machines that were found by the US military. Technical staff then secretly analysed the remains. Wright Field was also destined to be the base for the official US government UFO project when it was secretly launched some five months after the Roswell crash. This project continued until 1969, and was latterly known as Project Blue Book.

On the Foster Ranch the two airmen and Brazel spent all Monday loading huge amounts of the wreckage into a truck to drive back to Roswell. It was 2am on Tuesday 8 July when Marcel arrived back at the base and the Air Force intelligence officer took the opportunity to show the material to his family. Jesse Marcel Jr, now a doctor, recalls getting out of bed to view this amazing wreckage. He remembers how attempts were made to bend some of the metal with a sledgehammer, but these failed.

Later that morning Marcel and Cavitt met Colonel Blanchard on the base to decide what they should do next. Blanchard immediately sent the counter-intelligence officer back to the Foster Ranch to make the site a 'secure area' and to ensure that every piece of debris was collected. He also ordered him to bring Brazel back to town. Indeed, the rancher was placed under house arrest for a week. Cavitt took several military police with him and roadblocks were set up to secure the crash site. Major Marcel was ordered to fly with the remaining wreckage to meet with Roger Ramey and Thomas DuBose at Carswell and supervise its follow-on flight to Wright Field and the subsequent FTD scientific analysis.

Colonel Blanchard then met with Lieutenant Walter Haut, the Roswell base press officer, and dictated a press release which stated the incredible news that the remains of a flying saucer had been recovered locally. Haut himself then took this press release to the local radio station and to the local newspaper. By early afternoon the news was spreading far and wide, and at an incredible rate. Calls were coming in to the base from as far away as London asking about the authenticity of this amazing story.

As Major Marcel flew to Texas with crates of the remarkably light debris, the Pentagon and FBI were furious that the staff at Roswell had released information to the press and were trying to suppress the story. In Albuquerque, teletype operator Lydia Sleppy reported how she was forwarding the details of the crash across the west when the machine suddenly went dead. An FBI message then came through ordering her to cease transmission immediately. She was told that the information was part of a 'national security' matter. After that, the story never really took off.

As to what this wreckage really was, Marcel could only presume that it came from another planet.

When Major Marcel arrived at Carswell with the crates of wreckage that Tuesday afternoon, he was taken by General Roger Ramey into the map room, so that he could point out the location of the crash site. When he returned to the office, a bemused Marcel found a mass of debris laid out on the floor and was told that he was to be photographed alongside it. His job was to confirm to the press that this had now been simply identified as a weather balloon. A Carswell meteorologist was brought in and endorsed the diagnosis. Major Marcel was stunned, for he knew that the wreckage that had been found was not a weather balloon.

The Major has always claimed that Ramey told him this was simply a ruse to distract the press, and that Marcel should follow orders. In fact, nobody knew what the debris really was. Colonel (now Brigadier General) Thomas DuBose was in the room that day and supports Marcel's story. He said that the base had 'orders from on high to ship the material directly to Wright Field by special plane ... The weather balloon story was a complete fabrication designed to get the reporters present off Ramey's back in a hurry.'

By early evening on 8 July 1947 the short-lived story of the Roswell crash were disappearing. Photos of the 'balloon' were published in the newspapers and headlines wittily stated: 'General Ramey empties Roswell saucer'. The world's interest in this case died, but secretly the wreckage was being flown to Wright Field on a special flight as nobody yet knew what it really was.

The report to the FBI stating that – despite the cover-story – the Roswell wreckage had not yet been identified as a balloon.

At 6pm that evening a report to the FBI (which was secret until released by the US Freedom of Information Act 30 years later) explained how the debris resembled a balloon, but was not formally identified as such, even though the world was being told it was a balloon. The truth behind the Roswell cover-up was then hidden, until it was told by Major Marcel when he retired from the US Air Force in 1978.

Marcel said in 1978 that he felt obliged to reveal the facts. He carefully explained that the wreckage was truly remarkable and that he was unhappy with the continued pretence of his government after so many years. As to what this wreckage really was, Marcel presumed that it was 'not of this earth'. He was concerned with the possibility that an alien spacecraft had crashed in the New Mexico desert, and that the world was kept from learning the truth. Presumably the spacecraft was still locked away far from public view.

The UFO Crash

The Mystery UFO: The Military Involvement

FOR ONCE IN A UFO encounter nobody actually disputes the basic facts: an object did crash in the New Mexico desert. What needs to be decided is whether General Ramey told the truth when he later identified the object as a weather balloon with a foil metal radar deflector. Or was this just a way of silencing the media whose interest in the object had seriously worried the Pentagon? If so, then the next, more critical question is: what really did crash at Roswell?

General Ramey never spoke out about his role in this affair, but everybody else from the military who was directly involved at Roswell and Carswell during that 48-hour period tells a consistent story. Meteorologist Irving Newton is adamant that the wreckage he saw on the floor at Carswell prior to the arrival of the press cameras was definitely just a weather balloon. Even Major Jesse Marcel agreed with that fact, but insisted that the true wreckage had been switched while he was in the map room.

Thomas DuBose denies this. He says that the press were indeed falsely led to believe that the recovered debris had been identified as a weather balloon. He added that General Ramey ordered him to ensure that all of his men maintained silence on the matter. He also had to ensure safe passage of the wreckage onto Wright Field where the remains would be assessed. Yet DuBose was adamant in a 1991 statement that the wreckage they put on display, and which appears in the press photographs with Jesse Marcel, was the same debris that the officer had brought by plane from Roswell. DuBose says he was in charge of it from the moment he met the landing aircraft and it could not have been substituted.

Yet there seems very little doubt from its appearance on the photographs taken at Carswell that the material in

> *In 1994 the USAF was ordered to come clean and admit that they had lied in 1947 in claiming that the debris was from a weather balloon.*

Ramey's office comes from a balloon, just as the weatherman Irving Newton confirmed. So there is a significant discrepancy in stories.

Interestingly, the US Air Force were forced to review their records 47 years later as a consequence of an investigation by US Congressman Steven Schiff. He was acting as an ombudsman on the case for the GAO (General Accounting Office). This GAO enquiry resulted from public pressure due to the enormous interest in the case. As a result, in 1994 the USAF was ordered to come clean and admit that they had lied in 1947 in claiming that the debris was from a weather balloon. The USAF then admitted that they had not lied to cover up their recovery of an alien spacecraft, but because they knew the wreckage was part of a then top-secret experiment that had to be protected at all costs! Yet if the real debris was allowed to be photographed by General Ramey on orders from the Pentagon, how does this fit with their subsequent paranoia over protecting a military secret? Surely the last thing they would have done would be to show off the real remains of their top-secret device! Also, why was the truth not revealed in 1978 when Major Marcel first told the world it was a spaceship? By this time the once-secret project was out-dated and had been declassified as a result.

The Aliens Have Landed: The Prospector's Story

WHATEVER CRASHED AT ROSWELL has gained legendary status, not so much as a result of the fairly mundane bits of material scattered over Brazel's ranch, but because of the widespread belief that this wreckage was part of a spacecraft from another world. The main reason for this belief is the claim that the main part of the device

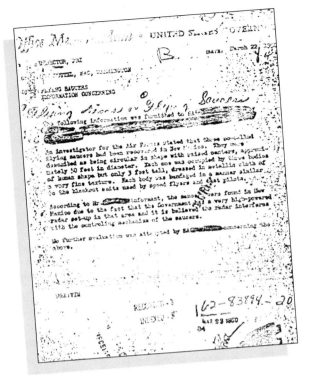

An alleged FBI memo drawing attention to an apparent retrieval of a UFO and its crew in New Mexico.

Yet there is some support for the theory that alien bodies were found. Glen Dennis, a mortician in Roswell, alleges that he was asked by the military base to produce a very small coffin. He went to check this odd request but was turned away. A nurse on the base told him that this was because they had the bodies of aliens recovered from the crash of a spaceship. Unfortunately, despite extensive efforts, no trace of this nurse has ever been found.

The most intriguing story comes from the widow of Oliver Henderson, a highly respected USAF pilot. Before his death he told his wife that he had flown the Roswell wreckage to Wright Field and that he had also taken the bodies of small, humanoid beings. He broke 30 years of silence after reading Marcel's confession, saying that it was no longer a secret. But he still requested her discretion until after his death.

A Black and White Film: The Evidence of the Cameraman

ERTAINLY THE MOST remarkable story associated with the Roswell case concerns the release in 1995 of a film that reputedly shows the autopsy on one of the alien bodies. This footage, in black and white and without sound, was purchased by a British rock music and video entrepreneur, Ray Santilli, supposedly from a former US military cameraman. This man, who was in his 80s, had sold it to help out his family as he became old and frail. He had kept the film in his possession since July 1947. The Pentagon had supposedly failed to claim it with the rest of his photographs and never realized that he still held it.

The footage does indeed show a room in which a strange humanoid body is cut open and its various organs removed. Other scenes depict large lumps of metal with symbols on them – supposedly the beams with the 'picture hieroglyphics' that were found at the Foster Ranch site.

Debate about the credibility of this autopsy film has been intense. Many UFOlogists and most of the key researchers in the Roswell case suspect that Santilli has been tricked. There are obvious practical difficulties in

fell elsewhere and that it was recovered, along with the alien crew, in a military retrieval exercise. None of the major people who were involved in the Roswell story have ever confessed to seeing either the second crash site or any alien bodies.

The first hint that there might have been a second site came from a couple who attended a lecture given by one Roswell enthusiast, Stanton Friedman. They reported how in the late 1940s a former neighbour, who had died in 1969, had told them a fascinating story. This man, Grady Barnett, was a soil conservation engineer who claimed to have been prospecting on the plains of San Agustin in 1947, 100 miles west of the Brazel ranch, when he came upon the wreck of the spacecraft. An archaeologist and some students were already present at the site studying the incredible remains of the craft. Small aliens with large heads and big round eyes were lying dead beside it. Shortly after Barnett arrived, the military came and took command, telling all the civilians to leave the site. This story has never been verified, despite extensive efforts to trace the archaeologists or one of the students. Several individuals came forward to claim involvement with this incident, but investigation has shown that they were not the people in question. Also, nobody living in the area of the supposed second crash site clearly recalls any reports, unlike the people of Roswell, where the affair is legendary.

The film stock carried markings on the side that Kodak agree might suggest it could have dated from 1947.

believing that the US government would allow a film of the wreckage of an alien aircraft and an alien autopsy to be kept in someone's home for 50 years. In addition, superior colour film with sound was used to record events, such as the first atomic bomb tests nearby, two years earlier. So it seems rather incredible that one man with a fairly crude black and white camera would capture such a momentous and unrepeatable process as an alien autopsy.

However, Santilli and one or two UFO researchers who have supported the cameraman's cause, note some positive evidence. The film stock carried markings on the side that Kodak agree might suggest it could have dated from 1947. Pathologists who have viewed the film have generally concluded that it shows a real body rather than a model or doll. Unfortunately, the film quality is poor enough to make judgement difficult.

It is difficult to substantiate what is on the film with the reports from the Roswell witnesses. The metal fragments seem to look too heavy in comparison with reconstructed pieces made under the guidance of people like Jesse Marcel Jr, who actually saw the real debris. The alien body is rather too human and lacks most of the detail described by witnesses.

This puts the authenticity of the autopsy film in doubt. On the other hand, the alleged 200-page autopsy report by Dr Frederick Hauser (see p.39) existed before the autopsy footage. The doctor's account of his surgery on an alien body mentions how human it looked, and his description is similar to the body seen on the Santilli film.

Optical physicist Dr Bruce Maccabee suggests that the recovery of an alien craft at Roswell might have led to a long struggle to decipher the unknown technology.

Mysterious Documents: The UFOlogist's Case

ROSWELL IS ONE OF THE UFO movement's major pieces of evidence. But why would the Pentagon wish to keep hidden such a momentous event?

According to nuclear physicist Stanton Friedman, a 'cosmic Watergate' has followed the Roswell recovery. He has investigated some mysterious documents that were sent anonymously on film to some UFO researchers during the early 1980s. These controversial files contend that a top-secret agency called Majestic 12 was created to mastermind the cover-up immediately after the Roswell crash. The US president was then only told after he took office. Some of the files purport to be briefing papers given to the president explaining the events of the New Mexico crash.

Many UFOlogists doubt that these mysterious MJ12 papers are authentic, although at least one reference to the agency has turned up in official government records. The US authorities deny any such body has ever existed and claim the file could have been planted in the archives by anyone. However, Friedman has collected much evidence to back his claims. He has revealed that many of the people named as participants in MJ12 during the 1950s appear to have led covert lives in which they may have participated in intelligence operations of a highly secret nature.

Optical physicist Dr Bruce Maccabee suggests that the recovery of an alien craft at Roswell might have led to a long struggle to decipher the unknown technology. If the craft was technologically many years ahead of our present knowledge, then it would have been virtually incomprehensible to the experts at Wright Field back in 1947. Indeed, it may still not be possible to understand, let alone duplicate, the technology of the craft.

UFO researchers argue that the cover-up has continued in order to allow the US authorities to retain alien information over its international rivals. They contest that scientists continue to unravel information from the wreckage of the recovered alien craft, although it could well be centuries before our technology allows us to appreciate the workings of this device. In the meantime, they say, the wreckage is being used for constant research, allowing the USA to keep ahead of all other major powers. No nation would ever wish to share that advantage with the rest of the world.

The Roswell debris, along with the remains of other crashed UFOs, is now said to be held in Area 51, a highly secret military complex in Nevada where top-secret aircraft are built and tested. The authorities have purchased the surrounding mountain areas near the base to prevent civilians from filming test flights even from great distances. Some intrepid hunters have succeeded in taking films, however, and videos depict extraordinary craft with amazing capabilities. Aviation experts say that the aircraft that are test-flown within this base are incredible, but have been built with technology from Earth. UFOlogists argue that they are built with the help of the evidence from the Roswell crash.

Balloon Bombs: A Journalist's Theory

NEW YORK JOURNALIST JOHN KEEL believes that the true source of the wreckage on the Foster ranch was neither a weather balloon nor an alien spaceship. He says that it was a bomb launched against the US mainland by the Japanese. Absurd as this theory may seem, it actually has some good evidence to support it.

During World War II the Japanese created what were called 'balloon bombs'. They were constructed out of parchment and light wood connected to high explosives, and then set adrift across the Pacific towards the west coast of the USA. Incredibly, some of them reached their destination and fell to earth up to 1000 miles inland. Because they did not wish the Japanese Emperor to know how successful these crude weapons were proving, the US government kept the flights secret. That was until spring 1945 when a group of picnickers in Oregon found a balloon bomb which detonated as they inspected it. Their deaths were the only ones on the US mainland as a direct result of enemy action during the war.

The balloon bombs became declassified as a result of this tragedy and Brazel certainly knew about them. The description of the Roswell debris is similar to these bombs, even down to the parchment with hieroglyphics that could have been Japanese writing. Perhaps such a bomb had been lodged in a crevice since the end of the war. Indeed, other undiscovered balloon bombs were

OTHER UFO RETRIEVALS

THE ROSWELL CRASH is by no means the only story of its kind. The existence of other cases where UFOs have crashed and been retrieved may well support its credibility.

In June 1908 something exploded over the tundra in Siberia not far from the Tunguska River. Whatever this object was appeared to change course in mid-flight. Its detonation destroyed huge areas of forest and killed many wild animals. Attempts to prove that it was a meteor or a small comet failed. There is also some suspicion from the evidence that it was a nuclear-powered craft of some description. No natural nuclear explosions occur, so if the suggestions that radiation emitted from this detonation are proved to be correct, it must have been an artificial nuclear device. But in 1908 atomic power had yet to be discovered on earth.

Another UFO crash was said to have occurred in Kingman, Arizona, during May 1953. Military personnel reported being taken to the site in buses with blacked-out windows, presumably to prevent them from finding their way back to the crash site. Once more small bodies of child-like beings with pear-shaped heads and large eyes were reportedly retrieved. These were taken with the wreckage to the Wright Patterson Air Force base, according to the stories. Various other death-bed confessions have been reported from personnel who apparently consider themselves free to speak as their life nears its end. These confessions refer to being present at autopsies, or seeing alien bodies inside crates in a secret hangar at Wright Patterson. But are these just imaginative tales?

One British military officer, for example, allegedly smuggled out of Wright Patterson an autopsy file in which a government scientist, Dr Frederick Hauser, described the alien bodies he examined in great detail. They were said to be 'eerily like humans' but much smaller in stature and with completely hairless bodies.

One of the most remarkable confessions came from Dr Robert Sarbacher, a scientist who headed the Washington Institute of Technology, and was a chief science adviser to the President during the 1950s and 1960s. Prior to his death he admitted that the US government had indeed retrieved alien craft and bodies of the crew. Sarbacher said that the machines were made of an unknown material that was 'very light but tough', and that the aliens were 'constructed like certain insects we have observed on earth wherein, because of the low mass, the inertial forces involved would be quite low'. What did he have to gain by lying?

CASE STUDY

The Man-Beast

WHEN THE ROGERS FAMILY moved into their farm at Roachdale, Indiana, it was to be a new beginning. Randy, Lou and their children set up a stock of chickens that would help them to be self-sufficient and to maintain a reasonable lifestyle. However, they had no idea that this small business would lead to a mysterious being paying them a call and almost wrecking their lives.

The family first realized that something was wrong when they heard pandemonium outside and rushed to find their chickens squawking in blind panic, and signs of slaughter all around. Something had attacked the birds but had not eaten any of them. It seemed almost like gratuitous vandalism and they call in the police to investigate. They agreed to keep a lookout for the attackers but admitted there was probably little that could be done unless the culprits were caught in the act.

The Rogers then maintained an ever more vigilant watch for the attackers, but this only added to the mystery. Randy spotted a large figure with matted hair silhouetted against the barn. It was just standing there watching their hens. It was similar in appearance to a huge gorilla, except, of course, that they knew that this was impossible, because there were no big apes living in the woods of Indiana. The creature's shoulders were very broad – making it appear as a powerful and terrifying beast. It also gave off a terrible smell.

Over the next few weeks the beast was seen on several further occasions. And once it was spotted loping off down the road. They also found indirect evidence, such as flattened bushes where a large creature seemed to have run through them. In the area where the beast had been seen there was the same stench as noticed before.

The chicken slaughter continued. Indeed, the attacks soon escalated, spreading to properties all over the region, with hundreds of birds' deaths eventually being

attributed to the attacks by this mysterious creature that nobody could ever catch in the act.

But an explanation proved frustratingly elusive. William Woodall, the local conservation officer, stepped in to try to resolve the situation for the authorities, but although he caught brief glimpses of the hairy beast, he never managed to get close enough to see what it was.

Lou Rogers said that it behaved almost like a ghost. On more than one occasion as it stood on their property, defying them to come after it, she said it appeared to be semi-transparent. The sky was visible in its body. It was very hard to explain.

Even when they chased it off into the bush across fields that were covered in mud there were never any footprints left behind. The Rogers, and Woodall, had all left their own tracks, but the phantom beast never left any sign.

The frustrated conservation officer bemoaned his complete inability to come up with concrete evidence to establish that a real creature existed. Yet he had seen it. The Rogers family were confronted by it too often to doubt it, and the dead chickens were proof enough that no ghost was to blame.

Then one night the Rogers had finally had enough. The creature was spotted near a trailer heading for the hen house. This time they were prepared and went out with a rifle determined to end the siege once and for all.

Closing in on the creature it was obvious what they were looking at – a large beast perhaps 2.4m (8ft) tall with a human build but covered in dark matted hair. Certainly it was not human in any understood sense of that word. In fact they could recognize it now for what it was. This was a bigfoot, an ape-like man-beast that has terrorized many parts of North America.

Taking no chances Randy Rogers aimed and fired. He had the beast at point-blank range only a short distance

> *Randy spotted a large figure with matted hair silhouetted against the barn. It was just standing there watching their hens. It was similar in appearance to a huge gorilla. The creature's shoulders were very broad – making it appear as a powerful and terrifying beast. It also gave off a terrible smell.*

Bigfoot allegedly caught on camera in 1995, by a forest patrol officer at Wild Creek, in the foothills of Mount Rainier, USA.

away and could not possibly have missed – yet the volley of bullets passed clean through the creature as if it were not even there. As usual the beast then loped off, almost seeming to bounce over the terrain, and disappeared into the woods. It was completely unharmed and seemed not to have even noticed the bullets that had been shot into its midriff. Although they had not even wounded the creature, as the lack of blood on the ground next morning proved, at least they appeared to have frightened it away. Bigfoot had apparently left the Rogers's farm and did not return. It was as if the beast was now seeking out new human beings to frighten and new places to haunt.

THE MAN BEAST · THE MAN BEAST · THE MAN BEAST · THE MAN BEAST
THE MAN BEAST · THE MAN BEAST · THE MAN BEAST · THE MAN
AST · THE MAN BEAST · THE MAN BEAST · THE
MAN BEAST · THE MAN BEAST · THE
THE MAN BEAST · THE MAN BEAST · THE MAN BEAST · BEAST ·
THE MAN BEAST · THE MAN BEAST · THE MAN BEAST · THE MAN

The Man–Beast

Myth or Truth:
The Folklore Dimension

ACCORDING TO AMERICAN BIGFOOT researcher Loren Coleman there have been reports of these creatures from so long ago that they are almost a mythology. In a paper published by the International Fortean Organisation (INFO) Loren Coleman argued: 'A vast folklore and a belief in a race of very primitive people with revolting habits is found from Northern California up into the Arctic ... Generally these subhominids are described as very tall, fully haired and retiring.'

The tradition was particularly strong at the Canadian frontier where trappers newly arrived from Europe often came across natives who warned of the dangers of hunting in the vast wilderness that confronted them. Thinking that at first that the natives were merely describing bears, they soon realized that there was a strong belief in something much larger and more intelligent – a being in fact that had human attributes but an animal-like appearance.

A vast folklore and a belief in a race of very primitive people with revolting habits is found from Northern California up into the Arctic.

Sasquatch, as it was called, was said to be particularly deadly to hunters because it was a notorious meat-eater. With its vicious strong teeth it could rip the flesh off the animals that it captured. Although there were no stories of humans being killed and eaten by these creatures, it was obvious that this was viewed as not altogether impossible given the strength of these huge beasts.

The other consistent feature of the myth was the claim that sasquatch always smelled very badly indeed. Natives spoke of how the rotting flesh of these victims of these creatures clung to their mouths, but the foul smell extended much further and was considered far worse even than the notorious smells emitted by a skunk. This unpleasant smell is also commonly detailed in more modern-day reports of encounters with the creatures.

There are over 100 different names for sasquatch in native American dialects. Amongst the myths told by different tribes, many speak of the magical abilities of the beast: how it uses mind control or telepathy, and can even make itself invisible. Other legends interpret the appearance of this 'secret race' as a warning of coming ecological disaster.

Such stories took on the air of folklore because none of the early settlers seem to have recorded any direct sightings of the man beast. For this reason they were considered simply as stories – spread by the native population – possibly to warn their children off from entering the forest alone or to prevent hunters from going onto sacred hunting land. The same principle applies even today with our own adults often scaring youngsters away from these areas by talking of 'boogey men'.

However, South American explorers did occasionally have more direct encounters. During the 1680s a group of Spaniards seeking gold in the Andes Mountains was reputedly attacked by a party of the man-beasts and there were casualties on both sides. They had been warned not to enter certain parts of the Colombian and Ecuadorian forests where the creatures lived but, as in Canada, had written off the tales as simply local superstition.

No Hard Evidence:
The Sceptical Approach

CSICOP – THE COMMITTEE for the Scientific Investigation of Claims of the Paranormal – is highly cautious regarding any bigfoot stories. It is their opinion that reports are a mixture of wishful thinking, exaggeration and misconception of normal wild animals. One of the key arguments used by the sceptics concerns the lack of physical evidence. While there are some reports of footprints and other potential signs that a

MAN-BEASTS WORLDWIDE

THE NAME 'BIGFOOT' is possibly the one by which these large man beasts are best known. But it generally only covers the reports from the forested regions of the north and west of North America, such as Oregon and California. In fact similar creatures have been reported for hundreds of years all over the world.

Indeed, the North American beast was known to the Native Americans. These original inhabitants called the creature 'sasquatch' – a word that is still used in Canada. Sightings suggested an ape/human cross according to many of the reports from intrepid hunters.

These same beasts are also reported as coming from a much wider area. In the vast continental reaches of the former USSR, for example, the creature is called 'almas' and the colour of the matted hair is said to be a lighter brown than observed in North America.

There are many similarities also with the yeti – or abominable snowman – which is said to roam the high mountain peaks of the Himalayas and is a sacred beast in parts of Tibet. Again the existence of this creature predates the arrival of western civilization and is well known among the local people. This snowbound creature is said to have white or grey hair.

Even the continent of Australia has its own bigfoot. The creature goes by a number of names, but it is most often referred to by the Aboriginal term, 'yowie'. Yowies are said to inhabit the rainforest of Queensland and the hinterland of the Blue Mountains in New South Wales. The existence of these creatures in a country that has been geologically isolated from the rest of the world for millions of years is fascinating. The remoteness of Australia explains why many of its animals, from the famous kangaroo and koala to thousands of smaller species, are so unique. If a near-identical man-beast is found here just as elsewhere in the world then this may well suggest that it is millions of years old and could have migrated all over the world from one common point of origin. Indeed humans did just that.

The study of the different bigfoot reports from all over the world is significant. For example, the colour of the hair changes in a remarkably appropriate way. It is white where there is a snowy background, dark brown where forests are the natural habitat, and light brown where sandy hills are common. It seems as if camouflage is the intention. Nature works in such a logical way, as seen by many different species whose skin colour helps them to blend into their environment, but people who have created myths tend not to. So is this evidence of the reality of this beast?

large creature has been in the area, including holes being smashed through bushes, no actual bodies have ever been recovered. There have also been no traces that could be properly analysed, such as droppings. In the quest for unknown animal life these are vital clues for the zoologist.

It is obvious that no new species of animal could ever be accepted without the zoologists being able to study the remains of at least one creature and then to be able to correctly match it to a species found on earth. If there really are colonies of these creatures in most mountainous and forested areas of the world, as the stories appear to suggest, then it seems inconceivable that not even one body has been found by the many hunters who have attempted to capture a bigfoot.

One of the key arguments used by the sceptics concerns the lack of physical evidence.

Sceptics accept that the man-beasts often inhabit areas that are quite remote but, with today's technology, where aircraft are capable of long-range surveillance and use infrared detectors that can sense the body heat of victims trapped amidst piles of rubble, it is hard to imagine how such creatures could escape detection so completely.

Some bigfoot hunters believe that the creatures are more intelligent than realized and may practise such human skills as taking their dead with them and even burying them for religious purposes. Yet even if that were true, there would surely be times where a creature, perhaps old or sick, would die alone and could not be 'rescued' by any other beasts in this way. Can it possibly be feasible that at no time over the past few hundred years has one single creature died in such a location where it could ever be discovered after death?

Only one pile of droppings has been found that might conceivably be from an unknown species, but no DNA sequencing was possible and its origin remains contentious.

Mountain Sightings: Hunter's Tales

WITNESSES OF THE MAN-BEAST in the Himalayas are very often highly respected. This is partly because the people that are climbing in these freezing conditions tend to be world-renowned climbers. Even Sherpa Tensing, who accompanied Sir Edmund Hillary on the first successful ascent of Mount Everest, claimed to have seen a yeti on an expedition in 1949.

An important case followed in 1951, when Eric Shipton led an expedition up Everest. He came upon a trail of footprints that led away up the virgin snow and disappeared over the cliff top. These footprints appeared to be from a large ape-like creature walking on two feet that had paused by their tents during the night, but then passed by without bothering the occupants.

Photographs of these 'yeti tracks' stunned the world when they were presented to the Royal Geographical Society after Shipton returned to Europe. An ice-axe had been laid alongside them to prove that they were much larger than any human print and would suggest a very heavy-set creature at least 2.4m (8ft) tall. However, it was noted that ordinary footprints can appear to grow quickly in snow because the sun melts the edges and causes them to collapse. This means that any prints not filmed immediately after they are made can seem larger than they really are. Yet here the tracks had not been present at sundown and were found soon after sunrise. There seems little doubt that they were always very large.

In July 1986, another mountaineer had an even more spectacular encounter. The famous Italian climber Reinhold Messner was 4,270 m (14,000 ft) up a mountain in Tibet when he saw something standing immobile behind a tree. After first thinking it was a yak he realized his error as he closed in. The creature was described by the mountaineer as 'not a man, an ape, or a bear'. He says

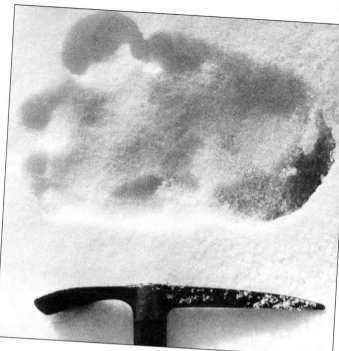

Eric Shipton took this shot of a Yeti footprint (shown in comparison with an ice-axe) during his 1951 expedition up Mount Everest.

it was well over 1.8m (6ft) tall and covered in shaggy greyish hair. This even covered the creature's face, although not as extensively. It stood on two legs, but ran in an ape-like posture crouched on all fours when the climber approached. Various other explorers have had similar encounters where they have often found tracks, but also occasionally seen the creature. There is a widespread belief in the existence of some unknown creature among the mountaineering community.

Modern-Day Visitation: Eyewitness Testimony

ONE OF THE COUNTRIES where much investigation has continued into these creatures is the former USSR. There are still vast areas of unexplored terrain, and several expeditions have been mounted by Maya Bykova, a Moscow Academy agricultural scientist, who has uncovered some impressive evidence of the creatures.

In 1991 there were numerous sightings of large ape-like beasts near Kargopol while a work crew was constructing a new road through the isolated area near Sosnino. The workers were mostly army conscripts and were not easily frightened. However, the barracks that were set up as a headquarters for the construction crew had been repeatedly visited at night by these large beasts before the most terrifying encounter took place.

On this occasion two of the creatures, seemingly having gained courage from their earlier attacks, invaded the barracks. They entered the mess hall and kitchen in full view of several soldiers and proceeded to put on a playful but intimidating display. The largest creature, about 2.4m (8ft) tall, stood on the stove and waved its arms about wildly. The smaller one, believed by those present to be the child of the first, leapt on a table and jumped about, much like a chimpanzee.

Both creatures were covered from head to toe in brownish matted hair and yet had almost human faces. They did not appear vicious but were apparently trying to scare the road crew. This they did very easily. Indeed some of the soldiers had to be treated for shock and one even lost his voice for several days. This was diagnosed as hysterical dumbness as a direct result of the experience.

After leaping about for a few minutes the two creatures raced off back outside and disappeared into the forest. A subsequent investigation found footprints in the snow that trailed off from the army camp towards the trees. In addition a few clumps of hair were taken from the scene for investigation by Dr Bykova. She was unable to identify any creature with which this sample might be associated.

Fronzoni argues from his research that: 'Bigfoot' finds you. You do not find it. If it wishes to avoid you then it will.

Fronzoni argues from his research that bigfoot finds you – you do not find it. If it wishes to avoid you then it will. He points out that most sightings have occurred by accident or when the creature has seemingly been attracted towards an unusual event in the woods. These events are often attributed to blasting or logging operations using heavy equipment.

To combat this problem he has hit upon a novel idea. Fronzoni takes his drum kit out into the Oregon forests and plays away, with the heavy refrain echoing through the snowbound emptiness of some of North America's wildest terrain. He hopes that this will arouse a sasquatch and provoke it to come and take a look at him, but up to now his experiment has not proved successful.

Others use a different 'lure'. Indeed Ron Morehead, who lives in the remote northern Californian woods, has released a tape for such a purpose. This contains some terrible, eerie voices recorded at his homestead late at night after they had been heard nearby for several successive days. The noises are not unlike guttural-sounding voices, gruffly speaking in a completely unintelligible language. They are animal-like but with a clear suggestion of intelligence and structure. Tests by linguistic experts at the University of Wyoming did not suggest that these sounds were a hoax set up by someone recording human voices at the wrong speed, which was an early presumption by some sceptics. Instead, many people believe that they might be the language of the sasquatch. And if you play them late at night in the woods then they just may attract a mate!

Local Tales:
The Bigfoot Pursuers

OFTEN THE QUEST TO FIND bigfoot begins with an innocent event, but then turns into a lifelong obsession. Henry Fronzoni started this way. On 1 August 1993 the Oregon man was driving near Skoocum Lake when he took a wrong turn. Going back on his route, he came upon an area filled with a terrible odour. He says that it was as pungent as a skunk but completely different. Getting out of his truck he was able to hear heavy footsteps crashing through the undergrowth in the distance. But these moved away and he never got to see what creature was causing them. Nor has he ever seen bigfoot since, despite long expeditions into the densest forest seeking one out.

Captured on Film:
The Film-makers' Story

PERHAPS THE MOST ASTOUNDING evidence for man-beasts is a piece of cine-film that was captured on 20 October 1967 by two hunters – Roger Patterson and Bob Gimlin. Two minutes of colour film depict a large, dark-haired, gorilla-like creature walking by some trees in the Six Rivers Forest area near Bluff Creek, California. It was taken at 1pm on a sunny day and as such is clearly defined. If this film is not faked then it is undeniable proof that bigfoot does exist.

A still from the legendary Patterson film of Bigfoot, which has yet to be disproved by sceptics.

The two men were no innocent passers-by. They were looking for the creature by following sightings in this location. Indeed, Patterson had already published a booklet attempting to document his theory that an abominable snowman was living in the local forests. As a result the hunters were riding through the most likely areas of the forest ready to capture the ultimate proof. When they came upon the creature, the men's horses went crazy and Patterson was thrown to the ground. Then, giving pursuit, hopping over logs and risking serious injury, they shot the footage that has stunned the world.

According to these two witnesses the beast displayed undeniable evidence of its intelligence. Indeed it even sat on a log and watched them for a time before they were able to start filming. In fact on the film itself the large creature seems to walk perfectly upright and saunter through the trees, stopping to glance back at the two men in what is an eerily human fashion.

Supporters of the footage as real evidence that bigfoot exists allege that mathematical calculations from the film prove that the figure must be about 2m (6ft 8in) tall and weigh in at over 182kg (400lb). Not many men dressed up in ape suit, they point out, could match those characteristics. Indeed, on one short sequence of the film the creature appears to display swinging breasts, indicating that it is probably a female. If so, then the likelihood of a human female being disguised to look like this creature is even more remote.

A trail of footprints was found at the site afterwards and plaster casts were taken. These show a thin but very large print over 35cm (14in) long. The markings are remarkably similar to several other alleged sasquatch imprints.

Fake Films: The Professional Cameraman's View

ONE OF THE MAIN REASONS put forward by those who doubt the film is the fact that the two men could easily have set it up. Their story indicates that they were expecting an encounter and they certainly used the outcome to good advantage in terms of the publicity that it generated for their continuing endeavours.

Possibly more significant is the gait displayed by the beast as it lopes across the edge of the forest. With a little practice a trickster could duplicate such motion. The stride pattern in the prints found at the site did not exactly match the one indicated by the motion of the figure on the film. Yet the way in which the creature lopes across the field of view is not exactly like either a human or an ape. Moreover, the way that the creature turns to face the camera is certainly rather too similar to an ordinary person for the comfort of many observers. However, it is very similar to eyewitness accounts of how the sasquatch moves.

The way that the creature turns to face the camera is certainly rather too similar to an ordinary person.

There are some who suggest that the figure is therefore simply an accomplice dressed in an ape suit. The two men vehemently disputed that idea and made the point that despite another 20 years of effort to film the beast this remained a one-off experience. If this had been a hoax, might they not have been tempted to try again and earn more money?

Films of man-beasts are not always what they seem. On 6 March 1986 Anthony Woolridge was walking through the Himalayas to raise money for charity when he came upon unusual footprints in the snow. Then he saw a large dark-haired creature standing erect and nearly immobile for 45 minutes. Woolridge took many photographs and on return to Britain it did seem as if he had captured impressive evidence. But on his return to the site three years later, he found that the creature was still there. It had merely been a very odd rock formation. In his state of excitement, exhausted and deprived of oxygen, Woolridge had interpreted it as something far stranger.

In 1997, biologist and wildlife photographer John Waters visited the Oregon woods to try to film bigfoot and investigate the Patterson film, He failed to get any footage of a real bigfoot and, in an attempt to create the perfect hoax, joined forces with a motion-picture special-effects expert. He designed a costume and Waters went 'on location' to Goat Mountain, Oregon, scene of several recent sightings of bigfoot. Despite his best efforts, the film still clearly looked like a man in a suit walking like a human and would not have survived much investigation, unlike the footage of the beast shot in the Six Rivers Forest. The Patterson film remains controversial, but has still not been disproved after more than 30 years.

SO WHAT DID HAPPEN?

You now have met some of the evidence that has been collected by both those who believe in the existence of man-beasts and those who do not. So what do you think invaded the farm at Roachdale?

● *Is there an unknown creature in many wilderness areas of the earth that has somehow avoided detection and left virtually no hard evidence of its existence? Is this beast a true 'missing link' – part ape and yet partly human? May it even be a distant cousin of ours that developed extreme physical size and strength rather than brain power, but with the prescence of mind to deliberately avoid confrontation with its one remaining enemy – humans?*

● *Or are the sceptics right to argue that the creature must be a myth without physical substance? If it existed there would surely be clear evidence of such a widespread beast. The legend of dark forests and monsters lurking within them is one common to cultures all over the planet. It is the basis of many fairy tales. Have we simply adopted these into our modern lifestyle and elaborated them with tall stories, the efforts of hucksters and various cases of wishful thinking, misidentification and imagination?*

● *Or, is there really a phenomenon here but one that is less solid than it might appear? Were the Native Americans correct in ascribing supernatural attributes to this creature? Has it failed to leave behind the telltale evidence of its existence because the man-beast stalks some kind of hinterland between reality and illusion? Might it even emerge from another dimension and return there after its visits? Or does the creature take on a brief semblance of life because we believe in it, but vanishes into unreality whenever it is challenged to prove itself?*

NARO researcher Tony Cranstoun snapped this ball of light that shot across the Great Hall at Chingle, England in 1996.

room called a 'hide' built into the wall. Here clergy hid for weeks on end to avoid capture by state forces.

On 25 December 1980 Gerald Main and noted Lancashire ghost-hunter Terence Whitaker kept a vigil near the hide and successfully taped some of these notorious rapping sounds. The noise was accompanied by a rapid drop in temperature within the house, a feature often reported during ghost sightings. Whitaker also saw what he termed as 'an indefinable shape' moving across the floor, which is believed to have been a ghost.

In January 1996 a team of NARO researchers, including Professor Ray Leonard, head of the Total Technology Unit at UMIST – at Manchester University – set up complex equipment at various points throughout Chingle Hall in an effort to capture solid evidence of the often reported phenomena. The equipment included video cameras and a continuous still film record of the location. While little of any substance appeared on the video film some electronic interference did occur. And the still camera recorded some very strange images.

At 2am on 26 January several of the team were in the Great Hall, scene of many of the past experiences, when a strange bluish white light appeared on the oak-beamed ceilings. Researcher Tony Cranstoun pointed his camera and shot two quick photographs, both of which

> *The noise was accompanied by a rapid drop in temperature within the house, a feature often reported during ghost sightings.*

successfully captured this ball of light moving across the room. This odd effect has not been identified and it is unusual in the sense that there were several different witnesses who saw the image as it was being photographed.

Efforts continue to monitor Chingle Hall in the hope that one day definitive paranormal evidence will be secured.

Electronic Ghostbusting: Computer Users' Evidence

THERE HAVE BEEN OTHER ATTEMPTS to harness ghostly forces by technical methods. During his 1980 visit to Chingle Hall, Terence Whitaker unveiled what he called a 'spectre detector'. This quaintly named device was tuned to emit a high-pitched note should there be changes in the ambient electrical field. It has long been thought by some researchers that ghosts appear whenever this energy field fluctuates and Whitaker certainly scored a spectacular hit. Moments before the rapping sounds and the ghostly vision appeared that night in 1980, the detector responded to a steady change in the electrical field within the room, its note rising continuously for some seconds.

Since 1980 other investigators have developed similar equipment and changes to the electrical field inside haunted rooms have been found from time to time. These usually happened at the same time as sudden drops in the temperature, for example. In addition, the increased use of computers since the mid-1980s has led to a flood of cases of 'electronic ghosts'. Often these take the form of unexplained interference on the computer screens and nonsensical messages being spelt out as if some force has taken control of the machine.

In one case from Stockport an office found that one computer screen was activating itself at night even when it was clearly switched off. It was picking up a flow of energy from an outside source and continued to do so when the plug was disconnected. This 'haunted office' had to remove this piece of equipment eventually to placate frightened staff.

A Cheshire technician who owned a home computer in 1985 claimed that it had started to reply to him by typing out messages on screen. It seemed to spell out replies to questions that he was thinking. At the same time as this phenomenon was occurring, objects started to move about his house in a rather more traditional form of haunting. The same happened to a couple living in an old cottage not far away, near Chester. But here the messages appeared to be coming from someone living in another century who seemed to send the message through some kind of 'time warp'. Again the house suffered a violent disturbance at the same time as the messages appeared. Furniture was turned upside-down while nobody was present in the room.

At the same time as this phenomena was occurring, objects started to move about his house in a rather more traditional form of haunting.

The possible electrical evidence of ghostly activity is now the source of much investigation by researchers. Some people think that it could hold the key to how these phenomena occur. Do they somehow distort the fabric of the universe to appear?

Supernatural Hallucinations: A Psychologist's Solution

FOR SOME YEARS psychologists have sought to explain ghostly activity as the result of hallucinations or unreal phenomena that are wrongly interpreted by the brain. In 1905 a doctor called Piddington published a comparison between pathological and supernatural hallucinations. The former occur when patients are taking strong pain-killing drugs that create a euphoric and dreamy state of consciousness. These pathological hallucinations tend to occur on the brink of sleep, with patients slipping in and out of reality. The patients also seem to experience frightening and usually shapeless images, sometimes quite monstrous in form.

On the other hand, Piddington found that people reporting ghostly apparitions described things very differently. They were usually awake, and could rarely sleep after such a shock to their system. The figures that they saw were rarely frightening or monstrous, unlike the images reported in drug-induced hallucinations. Indeed, they were nearly always completely recognizable as humans. Many witnesses said that if they had not known that the people they were seeing had died then they would never have realized that they were looking at a ghost.

Doctors Celia Green and Charles McCreery at the Paraphysical Laboratory in Oxford launched a more detailed study in 1965. They assessed hundreds of cases and found that apparitions differed from hallucinations in several other ways. Ghostly visions involved all the senses. People not only saw them, but heard and felt them, as well as occasionally smelling and even touching them.

Research was then done by London psychiatrist Dr Morton Schatzman. He found a star subject called Ruth who was able to create hallucinations of real people. These 'ghosts' sometimes just appeared and sat in chairs, talking to her. Eventually she learned to produce them to order whenever she wanted. These images were like ghosts in almost every sense, with one exception. The people who appeared to her were not really dead. They were alive and well and often hundreds or thousands of miles away from where Ruth was seeing them.

Schatzman joined forces with brain specialist Dr Peter Fenwick, based at a London hospital. They put Ruth in front of a machine that measured her brain activity. She was then asked to create a living ghost and to ask it to switch on a light in a darkened room. Ruth claimed it did so, and she could now see the room as being fully illuminated. Her mind behaved as if it was indeed in a lit room, yet she was unable to read a book in what was really still complete darkness.

In another test, Ruth was placed in front of a series of flashing lights. The brain cannot fail to respond to these because there is a physiological reaction in the optic nerves of the eyes and the brain. However, when Ruth made her ghost stand in front of the lights she believed it blocked them out. Her brain wave patterns responded as if she were no longer seeing the lights even though all the other people in the room could still see them.

So was this 'ghost' really in the room or not? The scientists were unable to answer such a seemingly obvious question and the nature of apparitions and hallucinations and the source of ghostly forms remains as confusing as ever.

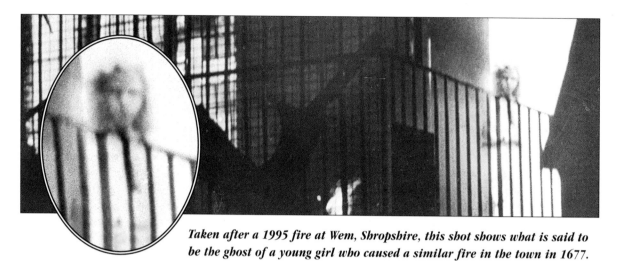

Taken after a 1995 fire at Wem, Shropshire, this shot shows what is said to be the ghost of a young girl who caused a similar fire in the town in 1677.

Trapped Spirits: The Message of the Medium

PSYCHIC MEDIUM DORIS COLLINS is amongst the best-known in the world. She regularly gives stage performances of what she perceives as a gift – her ability to channel information from people who are no longer living in this world.

How does she view the question of ghosts? According to Collins all of us comprise a physical body and a spirit body. Sometimes this gets confused with the term 'soul', although spiritualists, believers in a spirit life, say that there is a complex hierarchy that exists within the deeper self.

After death the physical body is cremated or buried and decays, but the spiritual being is freed from the ties that bind it to the material world.

On gaining freedom from the physical world the spirit is at first still close to the earth, and is perhaps reluctant to leave the people and the places that it knows well. Occasionally, when sudden death is involved or other very strong emotions are apparent, the person does not even appreciate that he or she has died and desperately seeks to maintain earthly contact. So some spiritualists think that hauntings and poltergeist attacks occur when the dead spirit tries to attract or maintain the attention of those they have left behind.

On gaining freedom from the physical world the spirit is at first still close to the earth, perhaps reluctant to leave the people and the places that it knows well.

According to Collins, most people after death quickly progress to a sort of heaven where a reality is constructed out of thought patterns and moulded to fit various spheres or worlds by millions of like-minded individuals. Souls that are on a similar wavelength congregate together and those that have done evil deeds find their new abode has a sombre appearance. But all spirits can progress upward even from the lowest realms of heaven. There is evolution of the inner self after death, just as all species of life on earth experience physical evolution.

It is the aim of a medium to pass on communications from those in the afterlife to people left on earth, as well as sometimes to bring comfort to those who are stranded on their way to heaven. Ghosts, in other words, may sometimes be in need of as much help as those left alive.

For centuries exorcists have been employed (and still are) by the Church to drive out evil spirits they think can possess buildings. But ghost rescue operations are more benign. Using prayer, positive loving thoughts and the attempts by a medium to contact the ghost a 'trapped spirit' is gently coerced to leave its earthly home and move on towards heaven.

Whether such moves are successful is open to question. Exorcists and ghost-rescuers believe that they perform a genuine act, while some psychologists suggest they achieve success because the occupants of the home believe in the power of such ceremonies. Once told that the ghost or evil spirit has left their home, they are less likely to misinterpret a continued 'ghostly presence'.

Energy Fields: Paranormal Enquiries

SURPRISINGLY, NOT ALL paranormal researchers who investigate ghostly activity are convinced that a spirit lives on after death. There are those who adopt a more pragmatic approach.

Peter Underwood is one such man. President of the Ghost Society, he has spent almost 50 years visiting haunted houses and seeking out proof of ghostly sightings.

Underwood has no doubt some cases involve genuine phenomena and that events that defy science are indeed taking place. However, he adds that he has never seen anything that has definitely persuaded him of an afterlife.

Underwood suggests that strong emotive events such as tragic deaths can be imprinted onto the natural fabric of the universe, through some kind of energy field. This may explain why there is evidence of electrical and magnetic field change when an apparition occurs. The signal is present within the atmosphere, and occasionally replays at random. Researchers suggest old stone houses may trap signals; others say natural energy fields in the earth might be somehow 'modulated' in the same way that we record images on video tape by changing magnetic signals.

Various ghost sightings occur where the figure seems to run through a set routine, such as walking down a corridor, as if the same image is being replayed time after time. There are even reports of ghosts that have been seen walking along an old pavement or floor that is at a lower level than the present one. These observations all fit the video signal theory.

Underwood suggests that a ghost may eventually stop appearing as its energy winds down over long periods of time. They will be replaced by new ghosts and these will create video replays hundreds of years from now to mystify the next generations of ghost-hunters.

So What Did Happen?

It is now your task to try to determine what happened on that October night in Butterflies nightclub. You have seen the evidence, heard the testimony and must judge the possibilities.

● *Was the whole thing a clever hoax, perhaps invented by persons unknown trying to publicize the club? If so, then how did it satisfy photographic experts and why did it miss out on its biggest opportunity – for the video to be screened on television? As it apparently passed the 'two-signal' test when examined by technicians for the BBC, is it likely that any hoaxer would not seek to maximize potential by involving a TV audience? Or did it start off as a joke, and was curtailed before it went too far? Is there any evidence of trickery when all parties named in this report appeared to satisfy researchers of their integrity? Or, perhaps, some unknown person hoaxed the management at Butterflies by faking the tape and planting it in the building. If so, this was a difficult and risky move and why would they attempt such a thing?*

● *If a hoax seems improbable, then could the ghost result from a mere accident? Was the tape not successfully wiped clean and does it show the remnants of an earlier camera shot recorded on another day when someone in a white shirt really did walk down the corridor and enter the cash office? When this faded image was superimposed by chance beneath the new film of an empty darkened corridor taken at night, did it possibly create the impression of a ghostly intruder? Was it pure chance that this occurred at the very moment when the alarm system was accidentally triggered?*

● *Was there a real ghost in the building – perhaps one of the workers killed half a century before when the premises were renovated? If so, then how did it seem so insubstantial that it could pass through a wall and door, and be substantial enough to trigger the alarm system? If this was a ghost then was it the spirit of someone hovering between earth and heaven, perhaps trapped in the in-between world unable to get over a sudden death? Or is the idea of some kind of energy form, like a video signal within the electrical fields of the earth, more acceptable? Could such a moving energy form pass through a solid wall just like radio waves might do because it was not 'really' there in a physical presence, but still had enough electrical energy to trigger the alarm?*

CASE STUDY The Mysterious Blob

ONE HOT SUNNY JUNE AFTERNOON estate agent Traven Matchett was working in the garden of his home at Mississauga, Ontario, Canada when the sky, quite literally, fell in.

Traven was painting fresh lines on the table tennis equipment that was kept outside. His teenage daughter, Donna, was nearby clearing leaves from the outdoor swimming pool. It was an idyllic and relaxing weekend scene, until it was sharply interrupted by a loud thudding noise. At first Traven assumed that his dog had struck a picnic table while it was playing nearby. He did not even look around. He did not feel he needed to be alarmed. That is not until Donna let out a scream!

The scene that greeted Traven was to haunt him for years to come. The centre of the picnic table was covered with huge flames that were flashing upward into the sky. A large gooey green mass sat in the middle of the wooden table.

The flames were themselves inexplicable. They jetted fiercely upwards, Matchett explained later, as if someone was below the table using a blow-torch. There was even a ring under the table where bits of the blazing blob had dribbled through the large wooden slats towards the patio.

The flames were reddish-orange in colour with streaks of yellow inside. They appeared to form a perfect cylinder and rose about 0.5m (1.5ft) into the air. Then the flames simply cut off. The tops of the flames were unlike any he had ever seen before. They formed a perfect sharp rim as if the fire hit an invisible barrier and was then stifled.

Donna reacted very quickly to the danger that surrounded them. She turned on the garden hose and pointed it towards the flames. With her swift action she managed to douse them before they spread. Now all that was left was the thing that had hit the table - what came to be known as 'the Mississauga blob'. It was a small fibrous mass and

was mottled green in colour. It weighed about 113g (4oz). It emitted a strong acetic acid (vinegar-like) smell that permeated the table for the next 36 hours.

This blob had apparently fallen out of a clear blue sky and come very close to creating a total catastrophe. If it had fallen a few feet in either direction Traven Matchett or his daughter might not have lived to tell the tale. If it had struck the house, which was just a short distance beyond the picnic table, it could have started a huge fire that would have been difficult to put out. The Matchett family had been very lucky indeed.

But what was it that crashed into their garden that day? This was to prove to be an enduring mystery.

Traven Matchett tried very hard to get someone to investigate what had happened that day. But he was soon to become frustrated. The offices of the National Aeronautics and Space Administration (NASA) were closed for the weekend. The local military base told him to call again on Monday. A neighbour, who was a pilot, recommended that he report the incident to Toronto airport.

Donna reacted very quickly to the danger that surrounded them. She turned on the garden hose and pointed it towards the flames. With her swift action she managed to douse them before they spread. Now all that was left was the thing that had hit the table - what came to be known as 'the Mississauga blob'.

The airport authorities were adamant that if it was a burning piece from an aircraft, the whole plane would have been ablaze, and there would have been a major alert at the airport.

Traven decided in the end to contact some local scientists at the Ontario Science Center. The only suggestion they could make was to report the blob to the media and see what happened.

It was to be the Monday before an inspector for the Ministry of the Environment came out to look at the damage for themselves. His explanation was that something on the table, possibly an ashtray, had caught fire and melted. The Matchetts carefully explained that everything else on the edge of the table was still intact and untouched. The intense fire had been very localised and only affected the centre of the table.

Eventually the local police did launch an investigation. But it was then that the mystery became even stranger. For the Mississauga blob was not unique. Three other local residents came to see the Matchetts and reported that they had also been attacked by falling blobs. One lived just a mile from the estate agent and his family. The other two were in nearby Brampton. The biggest of the blobs was twice the size of the one that fell on the Matchett garden. It was nearly 1.2m (3.5ft) long. Unfortunately, none of the other residents had been present when these blobs had fallen from the sky. They had merely discovered them in the garden after the incident was over. So they could not relate how long they stayed alight.

About a month after the Mississauga blob incident the American satellite Skylab fell from orbit and burnt up as it entered the earth's atmosphere. Some parts of it did not burn up completely and landed on earth. This led to speculation that the Missisasauga blob was part of another blazing satellite, possibly a Chinese one, that burnt up that weekend. But the problem with this theory, was that the three other blobs that had landed spanned a period of several weeks leading up to that June afternoon. So the pieces could not all have come from the same falling satellite, and for several different spacecraft to land in one small area on earth was virtually impossible.

In time, the case of the mysterious blob faded into obscurity. But such falling objects are in fact remarkably common, and the argument continues as to what they might be, and what causes them to drop from the sky.

This mysterious object fell onto a driveway in Wanaque, New Jersey, USA in the early 1960s. It weighed over 8lbs, 10 inches long and 5 inches wide, and was still warm when it was picked up by the homeowner. It has never been identified.

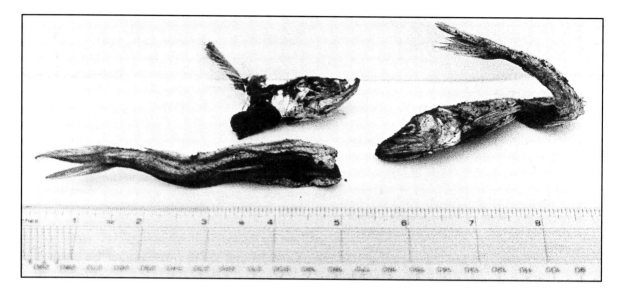

Other falls have included coins that rained down near a church, metal bolts, cans and bottles and even fresh kippers. The question is what causes these objects to get into the sky in the first place and then fall to earth?

Transported through Space: The Theory

POSSIBLY THE MOST BIZARRE explanation for these falling objects is that they are transported through space from one place to another. Surprisingly, there is some evidence to back up this theory. Bob Rickard notes that the sardines that fell on Plaistow were lined up in a formation that suggested fish who were swimming in a shoal. It was almost as if they had been plucked out of the ocean while swimming together, and suddenly transported into the air to be dropped in the woman's driveway.

Other cases exist in which animals have fallen from the sky many miles from their point of origin. At Nauplion in Greece in 1981 a shower of frogs fell from the sky. There were hundreds of them. The creatures were identified as coming from a species that were only found in Africa, thousands of miles away. However, the locals were less concerned about explaining how this remarkable event had happened, than actually coping with hundreds of croaking frogs that were keeping them awake at night!

Stranger still are a number of cases of living frogs that have been excavated from lumps of coal or stone during

In 1991, these fish fell from the sky on West Ham, London. They were identified as not being from local waters.

mining operations. If these rare and highly controversial stories have any basis in fact, it seems difficult to conceive of any way in which this can have occurred other than by teleportation. In other words, the frog or frogs were somehow 'moved' from one place in the outside world to the rock face.

That such phenomena might be possible is suggested by reports where car drivers have claimed contact with strange misty clouds. After driving into them they come out the other side at a point some distance from where they entered, as if these mists act like gateways. Journeys during these encounters have varied from a few yards to hundreds of miles, and at least a dozen well-recorded cases are known. These reports have come from all over the world and it might be significant that some of the falls of fish and other objects are often accompanied by misty showers of rain or ice.

Unusual Showers: What the Weathermen Say

THE RESEARCH TEAM that produces the *Journal of Meteorology* has studied a number of cases involving unusual falls of objects. One case involved showers of hay that fell from a clear sky. In several cases witnesses saw this happen. In June 1988 there was an episode at Marple in Cheshire where witnesses at a school saw the hay being sucked from the ground and swirled into a circular mass. The suggestion was that a form of whirlwind, which can occur on hot days, had the energy to pick up the loose hay. Although the witnesses, including a teacher and several pupils, lost track of the 'hay cloud' as it moved horizontally across the sky at about roof-top height, residents of a nearby housing estate a quarter of a mile away saw what happened next. Not knowing about the hay whirlwind they were amazed to see clumps of hay falling on their houses and the remaining cloud drifting overhead, still dropping its cargo as it travelled.

In this case the distance between the whirlwind sucking up the hay and then dropping it again was only a short one. Is it possible that stronger wind forces might be capable of collecting heavier objects, such as frogs or fish, taking them high up into the air and carrying them for many miles?

The possibility of long-distance journeys is certainly supported by another meteorological phenomenon known as 'dark days'. In these cases the sky goes suddenly very dark, even at noon, and afterwards a layer of yellow dust is found over houses and cars. It is known that these events occur when fine sand from the African desert is carried high up into the atmosphere by wind forces. It is then held there, swept long distances, to eventually fall like rain – blocking out sunlight and coating the ground.

But could frogs be carried such vast distances high in the sky and yet remain alive? There is clearly a big difference between fine sand particles being transported from the Sahara Desert and shoals of fish or colonies of living frogs being moved in this way.

Nevertheless, the possibility that whirlwinds and air currents might explain some cases of falls from the sky is a reasonable one, as there are relatively few cases of large objects crashing down.

Indeed, in some extreme cases where a whirlwind has crossed an area of land on a hot day, very heavy objects have been transported for short distances. In 1973 such a remarkable phenomenon lifted up the mayor's car from a driveway in a Staffordshire town and, after taking it a short distance through the air, dropped it back down again onto his garage, causing a considerable mess. So perhaps the transportation of a few frogs or fish in this way for longer distances is not quite so mysterious as it might at first appear.

TORRO (The Tornado Research Organisation that produces the *Journal of Meteorology*) notes that there are a large number of small whirlwinds or tornadoes in Britain each year. They are not as violent or destructive as those in other lands, such as the USA, and so often go unnoticed. But in fact the UK has more tornadoes per square mile than any other country on earth. It is not yet fully understood why this is the case.

So What Did Happen?

Now you must judge for yourself what is the cause of the mysterious blob that fell on the Matchetts' garden in Canada. There seem to be the three options open.

● *Were the authorities correct in suggesting that somehow a frisbee had been set alight and tossed blazing into the garden? Alternatively, there is the possibility that it was a homemade rocket that may well have been launched illegally. If so, is that what has happened during all the other similar cases?*

● *Could the falling mass have come from outer space, and was it possibly a kind of meteor or*

comet that had plunged through our atmosphere and caught alight through friction? Or had it fallen from a great height in this way but originated somewhere on earth, possibly having been sucked high into the atmosphere by wind forces? If so, what was the object that came down from the sky?

● *Or might the supernatural researchers have something when they suggest that more mysterious forces somehow take these objects from one point on earth (or the sky) and somehow convey them instantly to another location? If this is true the blob could have been teleported perhaps many miles to land suddenly on the table top in the Mississauga garden. If you believe this, once again, we still need to ask what the object was and where it came from?*

THE SWIRLING CROP · THE SWIRLING CROP · THE SWIRLING CROP · THE SW
SW · THE SWIRLING CROP · THE SWIRLING CROP · THE SWIRLING
CR RLING CR HE SWIRLING CROP · THE SWIRLING
OP · THE WIR RLING CROP
SW THE SWIRLING CROP · THE SWIRLING CROP · THE SWIRLING
CR · THE SWIRLING CROP · THE SWIRLING CROP · THE SWIRLING CROP ·

CASE STUDY

The Swirling Crop

GEORGE PEDLEY OWNED a large farm on the banks of the Tully River south of Cairns in Queensland in the lush sub-tropical paradise of Australia's Far North. Whilst walking past Horseshoe Lagoon early one January morning in 1966, he received the shock of his life. Rising from the reedy swamps was an incredible phenomenon.

Hovering just above the water was what appeared to be a large object shaped like a disc. It seemed to rotate and was emitting a gentle humming or buzzing noise. It appeared to be quite solid, but was very dark. There were no doors or windows or any kind of markings to indicate that it was some sort of constructed craft. He had never seen anything like it before.

The farmer edged closer. Unfortunately, the reeds and the marsh made it difficult for him to do this and he had to tread very carefully indeed. This land near the small community of Euramo was mostly agricultural. There was little else you could do with it because of the water that flooded across the area from the Tully as it wound its way towards the nearby Indian Ocean. You certainly would not find aircraft or helicopters attempting to land here.

As the disc rose into the air and began to disappear over the trees, Pedley could see that it was affecting the ground below. The reeds were being sucked upwards by

The reeds were being sucked upwards by some kind of force and were also being swirled into a circular pattern.

some kind of force and were also being swirled into a circular pattern. Although he had no idea at the time, he was witnessing the birth of the first recorded crop circle. Of course, this name was not to be adopted for several more years, and not by the Australian press but by the media in south-west England.

Once the disc had disappeared, George Pedley went as close as he dared to the side of the swamp. The remarkable effect was plainly visible. A circular area perhaps 6m (20ft) across had been swirled away. The loose reeds on the top formed a carpet or mat and these now floated in their new design on the calm surface of the river water.

The Tully reed circle became the talk of the local farming folk and this news spread to the paranormal researchers throughout Australia who sought an explanation. But to the people of the region there was often little doubt. They focused their attention on the possibility that an alien spaceship had landed near Euramo and the photographs of the damage that were quickly snapped by Pedley were the ultimate proof for which the world had waited. Of course, it was not to prove quite so easy to explain as that.

Possibly the first recorded 'crop circle' – taken after a 1966 UFO sighting in Queensland, Australia.

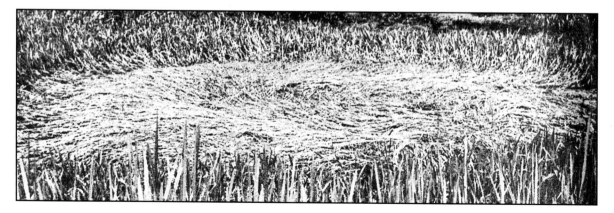

THE SWIRLING CROP · THE SWIRLING
CROP · THE SWIRLING CROP · THE
SWIRLIN   NG CROP
·THE SW   WIRLING
CROP   OP ·THE
SWIRLING CROP ·THE SWIRLING CROP

Was it a Hoax?:
The Investigator's Story

WHEN BILL CHALKER, a chemist and researcher into strange phenomena, arrived at the Tully River soon after these events, he was first obliged to eliminate the possibility of a hoax. It would obviously be quite simple to swirl these reeds into a circle and pretend that a strange craft had been responsible. However, there was a problem with this theory. As Chalker explained when I met him in Sydney before I flew on north into the rainforest: 'I doubt very much that anyone would have been foolish enough to carry out a hoax. There were crocodiles in the lagoon and the reeds are infested by Taipan snakes, which are among the most deadly on earth. You would need a pretty good incentive to risk those sort of dangers just to create a few marks in a swamp.'

Tests on the reeds afterwards had provided no evidence of radiation or fuel residue, but the crop had died very quickly.

Chalker had found no evidence of a motive. Neither did I. I talked to Pedley's family who backed his story. Everyone I met in the Tully River area was convinced that the swamp circle was genuine. They had good reason to believe that. It was not unique. Indeed, as I discovered, similar marks appeared in the swampland quite often during the summer months, of which, in Australia, January is one.

I talked to people at the Flying Doctor station in Cairns. They flew over the area quite regularly and had seen patterns formed in the trees. They thought that the weather could be responsible through what they termed a 'Willi Willi'. This is a kind of rotating whirlwind that forms on dry hot days as a result of air currents and. It was speculated that this might get 'bogged down' in a swampy area, producing the flattened effect of the reeds as the normal sideways force is pressured downwards. Whatever the truth, the marks were common enough for the general opinion that there had to be a natural explanation.

Some locals were more willing to consider the possibility of alien forces. The precision of the marks was cited. I was reminded that a whirlwind would ordinarily leave a ragged trail, not sharp edges. Tests on the reeds afterwards had provided no evidence of radiation or fuel residue, but the crop had died very quickly and the marks were destroyed by the prevailing winds within days.

A Queensland UFO team had set up a monitor on the area after the circle had first appeared. This featured automatic cameras that were geared to activate should anything move in the swamp. One day, almost exactly two years after the first circle appeared, the system was triggered. When researchers checked the site they found a new circle in the reeds and eagerly dispatched the film for processing. But it was never returned. In fact, according to the laboratory it never even arrived and seems to have vanished in transit.

Heading into the mountains that overlook the area I met some native Australians. These Aborigines told me that there are 'spirits' that are seen in the air and have been known to their people for thousands of years. When visible they often form orange balls of light. As I headed deeper into the Queensland rainforest I found a local Australian couple who produced artwork of the spectacular wildlife and sold this to people who passed by in their cars. They knew of these 'Min Min' lights, as they are called, and had seen them several times flickering above the trees. They presumed them to be some kind of natural phenomenon. But they were very real. So were they connected with the swamp circles?

The Mystery Circles:
A Farmer's Tale

CROP CIRCLES ARRIVED IN BRITAIN 14 years after they had first appeared in Australia, in the summer of 1980. The first person to discover them was John Scull, who grew oats in a field near Westbury in Wiltshire. John Scull explained: 'I first found a circle in my fields in May. But at the time I had no idea what it was. I just assumed that the weather was somehow to blame and never even reported it. I harvested the field and then forgot about it. But in August two more circles were found. This time I decided I had better

This crop circle 'pictogram' formation at Alton Barnes, Wiltshire, appeared in July 1990.

Age' community seized the opportunity and promoted the circles as the creation of 'sky gods' in a short, and at first largely unsuccessful, attempt to gain national press attention.

Meanwhile, Probe put an investigation into operation. They established through questioning local people the precise times and dates when the circles were formed. These were found to be 21 and 31 July. They took samples from the oat fields and had them analysed by the university in Bristol. There was no sign of any radiation or fuel residue. The crop was undamaged, was merely gently flattened, and had continued to grow normally. The team then consulted with physicists and meteorologists in their attempts to find an answer to how these circles occurred. They noted that other areas of rough damage in the same field were obviously wind damage.

In the end Probe concluded: 'The oats were flattened by air pressure or pressure of a similar nature.' They flatly rejected the emotive talk of aliens and sky gods and said that a natural phenomenon was to blame. Unfortunately, this cautious approach was soon to be forgotten by the mad rush to promote the crop circles as a huge new mystery. Indeed, Ian Mrzyglod and most of his team stopped their research in disgust because what they regarded as a fairly explicable phenomenon was blown out of proportion by the world's media. Thousands of supernatural researchers were also to turn searching for crop circles into both a farce and a money-spinning business.

let people come and take a look before I cut them down.'

Ian Mrzyglod of the Bristol strange phenomena research group Probe arrived on the scene on 16 August and took the only known photographs before the fields were harvested by John Scull. He notes that the two circles were 'about 91.5m (300ft) apart and were of similar size, one slightly smaller than the other but both around 18m (60ft) in diameter. Neither of the depressions were exactly circular but they nearly were. The beds of the nest consisted of flattened oats although there were small patches still standing at varying heights up to 1m (3½ ft) tall.' The circles were like holes cut by giant cookie cutters stamping onto the ground from above. The edges were sharply delineated with a border of erect crop. They certainly looked quite mysterious. However, the connection with the little-known and long-forgotten episode in Australia some years previously was not immediately evident.

Although there was a brief local press item, the 1980 circles got little attention compared with the global furore that was to follow in later years. But the nearby town of Warminster had once been very famous as a centre for UFO activity. During the 1960s people had gone there to skywatch after many local sightings of UFOs, and with the circles there was an opportunity to regain some of the attention the town had lost since then. So the Wessex 'New

> *The circles were like holes cut by giant cookie cutters stamping onto the ground from above. The edges were sharply delineated with a border of erect crop.*

Cosmic Messengers: The Engineer's Findings

IN 1985 COLIN ANDREWS, an electrical engineer from Wessex, where the circles were forming, became interested in the mystery of how crop circles were formed. This was after several more summers had brought further, isolated, crop circles to

British fields. He joined forces with pioneer circle hunter Pat Delgado, who first involved the UFO fraternity by writing articles in 1982 and 1983 for the magazine *Flying Saucer Review*. Andrews and Delgado published many papers and worked feverishly to interest the local, then national, and ultimately international media in their activities. They set up monitor sites at places where circles had appeared (initially just in Hampshire and Wiltshire but soon to spread across the UK and the world). The pair began to gather teams of like-minded supporters.

In July 1983 the circles first achieved serious national press attention when half a dozen patterns appeared in a more complex design. They formed one large circle surrounded by four satellites like a telephone dial or petals on a flower. Over the coming summers, these signs of an intelligent being or beings at work saw the patterns become larger, more frequent and even more spectacular in appearance.

By 1989 Andrews and Delgado produced a book called *Circular Evidence*. It took the world by storm. It was not the first publication on circles. BUFORA council member Paul Fuller and myself had published a booklet through that group called *Mystery of the Circles* in 1986. This was expanded to a full-length book called *Controversy of the Circles* and became the most successful publication the group had ever known, going through seven reprints in a year. However, it had attempted to develop the work of Ian Mrzyglod of Probe and show that the circles were natural phenomenon and not of alien origin. As such it was virtually unknown to the general public who really found the exotic and 'cosmic' ideas about circles far more exciting.

Andrews later continued investigations on his own. He then moved to America to continue his campaign when the British media lost virtually all interest in circles about 1992. But he has remained a staunch defender of their fantastic nature. He has even spoken about them to a United Nations sub-committee.

He helped coin the phrase 'pictogram' to describe the new developments in the circles mystery occurring after 1990. This was when mundane circles, however big, were replaced by crop circles that included snail, whale and spider pictures, and even highly complex geometric patterns. There was no question that these were not the result of swirling winds. In response Colin Andrews was quick to say that his rival's theories were discounted by the

If the circles were not caused by wind it did not automatically mean that they were the result of alien forces sending messages to earth.

evidence. But, of course, if the circles were not caused by wind it did not automatically mean that they were the result of alien forces sending messages to earth.

Colin Andrews met with the Hopi Indians in the American West. They claimed to recognize some of the symbols found in British crop fields and argued that they were a warning of how the earth spirit was unhappy. Ecologically minded researchers saw this as evidence that the circles were a cry for help, or even a reaction of the planet itself to the poisoning of the environment.

Andrews was less specific in his pronouncements but said that he favoured 'some form of intelligence' and an 'aerial entity' that used 'unknown forces'. Many people were to agree with him.

The Plasma Vortex Theory: A Meteorologist Speaks

B Y 1989, WHEN THE MEDIA discovered crop circles in a big way, a Wiltshire meteorologist called Dr Terence Meaden joined the furore surrounding the attention given to Colin Andrews, Pat Delgado and the newly formed crop circle investigation societies that sprang up in their wake.

Terence Meaden was no stranger to crop circles. He was consulted by Ian Mrzyglod about the first ones that appeared in Westbury in 1980 (ones that even Pat Delgado had not seen). As a specialist in tornado damage, he had concluded then that a whirlwind of some sort was to blame. After Mrzyglod left the field because many of his colleagues in the paranormal research field were hostile to his cautious approach, Dr Meaden joined forces with Paul Fuller. Fuller was a Hampshire statistician and became BUFORA's new champion of the circles mystery. He was in agreement with Mrzyglod in that he felt the phenomenon had no exotic explanation. He became an ally to Meaden, endorsing the scientist's views to the UFO community, while also investigating many circles first hand. Fuller also set up one of the first serious crop circle magazines called *The Crop Watcher*.

As the circles became more complex, Dr Meaden's initial theory that a fair weather stationary whirlwind was to blame started to lose credence. These small tornadoes occur on hot summer days, and are indeed the 'Willi Willis' referred to by the flying doctors in Cairns as a possible cause of the Tully reed circle. The meeting of hot and cold air in the lee slope of a hill causes the rotational force and if trapped in a cornfield could remain stationary for its short life and produce a simple crop circle. But such a phenomenon could not provide five circle formations, let alone pictures of whales and dolphins. So Colin Andrews and his supporters became very excited when the circle mystery developed further.

Meaden then suggested a new phenomenon – a form of electrified vortex that turned the surrounding atmosphere into a plasma. This glowing energy could possibly be seen as a ball of light. The electrical field could create 'satellite' patterns. But, of course, the pictograms were beyond such scientific rationalization.

Unfortunately for Terence Meaden his successful creation of the plasma vortex theory coincided almost exactly with the new development in the formation of the circles. Inevitably, science in general then struggled to find his ideas acceptable. While a conference was staged in Oxford in 1990 and Japanese physicists in particular later set up research projects that provided some evidence that a plasma vortex could exist, Meaden's theories were largely forgotten as the tide of 'cosmic message' speculation filled the media with the arrival of the pictograms. He retired to France soon afterwards. His critics then took pleasure in saying that he had given up, but he had done no such thing. He is still investigating crop circle data and convinced that a vortex explains the simpler cases. As for the rest, he is sure that they result from hoaxes.

Meaden's plasma vortex theory had more success in persuading some UFO researchers that he was onto something. Paul Fuller went on to write a book re-evaluating some rotating, glowing UFOs where no circles had formed as being sightings of such a rare meteorological effect.

The Fake Circles: The Hoaxers Confess

I N SEPTEMBER 1991 the crop circle mystery was dealt what appeared to be a final blow when two Southampton-based artists, known as Doug and Dave, confessed that they had made some of the circles. The two men approached a national newspaper who filmed them faking a small circle in Kent. They used

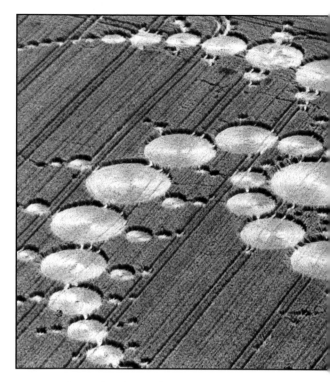

Messages from the skies? This elaborate series of circles appeared at Windmill Hill, near the sacred site of Avebury, England, in 1996.

a wooden board and rope to flatten the circle without leaving footprints or destroying the crop. Then Pat Delgado was shown the circle and he failed to realize that it was a fake. Once the truth was known, the mystery surrounding the crop circles faded. Not long before, Terence Meaden had been seen on camera seemingly impressed by another circle that later turned out to be a hoax. It appeared as if all the circles may well have been faked.

Doug and Dave claimed that they had got the idea after seeing the reports about the Tully circle while one of them was living in Australia. This one had not been faked, or at least not by them. But back in England they decided, as a joke, to put circles in the occasional field and see what happened. It took some years for the trick to catch on, but once it did they spent each summer carefully faking new circles to keep the mystery going. As time went by they felt they had to create new versions. Also when Dr Meaden came up with the weather theory they were forced to invent more complex patterns so that this theory would be discredited.

Now, in 1991, they had decided to retire. But they knew that other people had joined in the fun and were faking circles as well. Of the 2000 circles reported before

out the words 'We are not alone', perhaps forgetting that if aliens had really put it there it should have said: 'You are not alone'.

Even before Doug and Dave came into the open and destroyed the media interest in circles, *The Crop Watcher* had warned that hoaxing might be far more common than was being realized. These words were to prove very prophetic. Unfortunately, they were largely ignored and all circle researchers were perceived as being very gullible by much of the world's media.

Seeing the Light: A Farmer's Story

GEORGE PEDLEY MAY HAVE BEEN one of the first, but he was not to be the last person to see a crop circle forming. After midnight on 10 August 1989 Wilfred Gomez was driving on a small road on the Isle of Thanet in Kent when he saw what he termed as a 'solid hurricane of light'. This was a rotating white column that had a fuzzy top but a firm base, and was tinged with an electric blue colour.

Winding down his car window to look at the object, the driver heard a faint humming or buzzing sound coming from the light which appeared to be quite stationary, even as it rotated. After a few seconds the glow vanished and the noise stopped at the same moment.

Approaching the field over which the object had hovered, Mr Gomez walked inside and in the moonlight found a small circle, and then further in the field a much larger circles which was similar to the crop circles he had seen on television.

their confession, they had been responsible for about 200. But what about the many others?

Serious researchers had long known that hoaxing was taking place. It was too attractive to fraudsters, especially with the increasing media interest and the crowds of researchers and tourists that flocked to the West Country to view their handiwork. Ian Mrzyglod had exposed the first one in 1983, when one national newspaper paid a farmer to fake a five-circle pattern in an effort to catch out a rival paper. The other paper ignored it and the first paper quietly forgot about what they had done. As far as the public was concerned this was just another 'real' circle, until the UFOlogist unravelled the truth.

Paul Fuller and his colleagues at *The Crop Watcher* later exposed many more. By 1990 there were teams of hoaxers who were deliberately playing games with the crop circle community and working to a far more sophisticated strategy than Doug and Dave. Sometimes they daringly laid circles close to watch sites. Some were trapped on cameras. Others were simply caught in the act.

In other cases, the clues about hoaxing were rife. The villages of Littley Green and Fakenham were rather obvious locations for circles to appear. A message in crops spelt

When the sighting was investigated, the local farmer commented that his field was plagued by 'whirlwinds' and on several occasions he had found blighted areas where his crops were damaged.

When the sighting was investigated, the local farmer commented that his field was plagued by 'whirlwinds' and on several occasions he had found blighted areas where his crops were damaged. These areas had appeared in the aftermath of these rotating winds on days when it was hot and calm. Two or three times he had even witnessed a whirlwind lifting clumps of freshly cut crops into the air and dropping them down again. Also, the local RAF base at Manston confirmed that the location was well known for generating 'dust devils' in late summer. Because of these, they stated, they steered their planes away from the updrafts to avoid any dangerous situations.

This case, like many others that have been put on record by startled witnesses, gave reassurance to people on both sides of the debate. Those who believed that an alien force was creating the circles argued that it was clearly a UFO that had been seen. Those who favoured the weather theory took note of the clues that suggested that this was not only a form of whirlwind but one that generated an electrical field, causing the air to glow. It was, in effect, one of the plasma vortices that Dr Meaden had suggested. Indeed, as they pointed out, electricity power lines crossed the field. Perhaps this helped the plasma to form, as there would be ambient electrical fields. At the same time the cables would have made the landing of a large alien craft very difficult indeed.

In the summer of 1996 a ball of light was filmed by a video camera. It was apparently floating above a field in Wiltshire where circles were supposedly formed at the same time as it was visible. The similarities with the 1989 case are clear. By 1998, however, evidence was mounting that this film could well in fact be a clever hoax using computer graphics technology.

Historical Circles: The Editor's Investigations

P AUL FULLER, STATISTICIAN and editor of *The Crop Watcher*, has specialized in seeking out cases of crop circles that could not have been hoaxed by Doug and Dave. By their own admission they faked their first one in 1976 and only got the idea from the Tully circle in Australia. So any that appeared before then were not their handiwork. It is also unlikely that anyone else was faking circles on a regular basis before the media discovered them and gave a big opportunity for tricksters to get publicity.

Fuller has scoured old scientific journals, looked through folk records, and surveyed aerial photographs taken in the early days of flight when mapping from the air was in its infancy. Over 150 cases of crop circles have been discovered prior to the Tully case, and quite a few of them even predate the 20th century.

One of the earliest reports is of a circle found in a field at Assen in Holland in 1590. But possibly the most intriguing is an old woodcut which is dated as being from the year 1685. The woodcut describes circles that appeared in a field in Hertfordshire in August of that year. The crop was laid down in such precision that the legend says the devil was responsible, and the woodcut even has the title 'the mowing devil'.

Other cases include an eyewitness description of a circle that formed in France in the late-19th century. The phenomenon responsible is described as being like an invisible curtain of wind.

Indeed, there are even reports from the same area of Wessex where circles later came to such attention. These were recorded as 'saucer nests' and assumed to be the result of UFOs that landed in the early years of the flying saucer controversy. One eyewitness account from a field situated on the slope of a hill near Warminster (where 25 years later circles formed with regularity) told of how the crop was flattened by a gentle wind-like phenomenon that was unseen by the witnesses. The field simply swirled into a circle just 'like the opening of a lady's fan'.

There seems to be no doubt that there have been circles for hundreds of years. But none of these historical cases ever describe the creation of anything more dramatic than a single, simple circle. There are no multiple formations, let alone pictograms or images of spiders, whales, or other creatures.

Supporters of the weather theory believe that these older cases virtually prove that there must be a natural phenomenon that has always been responsible for creating a few real circles each summer. It seems less likely that any aliens or authors of cosmic warnings about the fate of the earth would have made these circles only to be ignored by everyone for centuries.

The Crop Circle Debate: The Die-hard Researchers

A LTHOUGH THERE IS VERY little media interest in crop circles nowadays, the admission of hoaxing by Doug and Dave in 1991 only ended the then strong press coverage. It did not end the subject. Indeed, remarkably, several crop circle groups still thrive and the original three crop circle magazines founded at the height of the publicity are still published. The CCCS (Centre for Crop Circle Studies, which publishes *The Circular*) still holds well-attended conferences and investigates dozens of new circle formations each year, mostly in the Wessex counties where the majority continue to appear. But circles continue to appear all over the world at the rate of about 200 per year on average.

The approach to hoaxing is more cautious than it used to be, with most researchers accepting that it plays an important role in many of the cases investigated. The difference is the explanations that are given to the circles that are no hoaxes.

The Crop Watcher still thinks that the vast majority of circles (and all the complex patterns) are fakes, whereas just a few simple circles each year result from weather-related causes. But even with this thinking there are changes afoot. In 1998 the magazine was taken over by its new editor, Peter Rendall, although Paul Fuller still retains his involvement after 10 years. Rendall has announced that he will be more amenable to publishing any well-argued research regardless of the theory it promotes, and that the magazine will no longer just support Meaden's research without question. Nevertheless, his own opinions seem to be quite similar to Fuller's. Indeed Rendall became involved in August 1989 when a local woman saw a whirlwind in a field near the remand centre at Pucklechurch in Avon. He quickly went to the scene and discovered that several rough crop circles had been left in its wake.

On the other hand the CCCS are clearly more willing to consider theories that might still be termed exotic. They seem less keen to reject the reports of pictograms and animal pictures in fields, and have also promoted research carried out by an American plant scientist who studied soil samples from many circles and allegedly found that their chemical composition had altered in as yet unexplained ways. This, they feel, may suggest that some kind of unknown energy field might somehow be associated with the formation of the circles.

Paul Fuller, however, has noted that as no distinction was shown between real and hoaxed circles, and several of the samples came from apparent fake circles, the results of this research are at best ambiguous.

The debate rages on and has even attracted a team from Florida in the USA, who have used high-powered laser lights in an effort to 'beam up' to the originators of the circle marks and urge them to make friendly contact. Another researcher from California has bought a field for several successive summers and carved out his own messages of contact in the hope that replies will be sent back to him. To date the closest he has come to success was when the symbol for a disabled toilet was found etched into a nearby field.

So What Did Happen?

This is a case that has stirred up a major controversy and there are fiercely divided opinions as to what really happened. Here is your chance to decide the answer.

● *Was the Tully circle in Australia faked by some brave bushman ignoring the local wildlife and simply hoping that his handiwork would be spotted before the wind blew it out? If this was the case, then the dark rotating disc shape that George Pedley claims to have seen creating a circle needs explaining. And why was it placed in such an out-of-the-way location rather than somewhere the media could have filmed it and readily given the publicity that was presumably sought?*

● *Was this object a spacecraft from another world, or the product of some other intelligence that was intent on telling us to mend our ways, or our earth*

will be destroyed? Alternatively, there is the theory that the spirit of the earth is somehow upset by our environmental folly and is making signs to us in the form of crop circles. Also, are such visitors creating the most visible sign possible by laying out patterns in our fields? If so, why start with a circle that was so obscure in its meaning?

● *Or are the supporters of the weather theories correct in arguing that a natural phenomenon produced by rotating wind has for centuries every now and then left circles on the ground during the brief moments of its existence? Can this sometimes electrify the air and create a glow? Could the dark disc shape that was seen in daylight have resulted from loose debris such as dirt, reeds or water spinning around in the centre of the whirlwind? One also needs to consider whether these circles, and the natural forces that create them, have always been interpreted in supernatural terms by the people of the day – so that they become Aboriginal sky gods, mowing devils or today's cosmic messengers.*

RETURN FROM DEATH · RETURN FROM DEATH · RETURN FROM DEATH
M DEATH · RETURN FROM DEATH · RETURN FROM
DEATH · RETURN FROM DEATH · RETURN
FR · RETURN
RE EATH · RETURN FROM DEATH · RETURN FROM DEATH
· TURN FROM DEATH · RETURN FROM DEATH · RETURN FROM

CASE STUDY Return from Death

THE BATTLE WAS RAGING FIERCELY, but Jacky Bayne was not deterred by the noise and smoke. He had been drafted into Vietnam to do a job and he was intent on doing just that. After a while the soldiers got used to the constant fear and tension. In some ways it was worse when nothing was happening because then the North Vietnamese Army (NVA), or 'Charlie', as US troops referred to the enemy, might ambush them at any moment. At least when there was conflict it was easy to see where the bullets and the mortars were coming from.

Jacky marched on through the undergrowth, glancing left and right to detect any sudden movement in the long reeds. It was 6 June 1966 – 6.6.66. The number 666 was the number of the beast on the Day of Judgement in the Bible, making that day seem all the more ominous.

The battle noises seemed some distance away, so Jacky felt there was no immediate danger. But it was hard to be sure. Suddenly the sounds of gun fire got much louder, and before he could react to this, Jacky felt a searing pain as a bullet hit his hand near the thumb. The wound started to bleed quite badly, but the shock dulled the pain and kept his mind clear. Jacky knew he had to press on and get out of the area which was under attack.

Jacky took a step forward and was about to move ahead purposefully when he heard the noise that all US soldiers had been taught to dread. It was the rushing, whining, screeching sound of a rocket missile soaring through the air and, from the way that the noise was reaching a climax he figured that it was heading straight for him.

The missile landed only a short distance from Jacky and exploded with such ferocity that he was thrown backwards through the air. He hit the ground hard and immediately lost consciousness. Luckily the force of the blast had propelled him well clear of the crater created by the missile, and the other rockets and gunfire that had now zeroed in on where he had been.

> *He thought to himself, I have just been blown up and I ought to be in terrible agony, yet I feel comfortable and relaxed. Jacky wondered briefly if he was dead and had gone to heaven.*

It was impossible for Jacky to tell how long he lay on the ground. It could have been a few minutes or it may have been a couple of hours. But as he started to come to, he realized that an extraordinary calm had descended on the battlefield and it seemed as if the fighting was over. Had Charlie been defeated? Such questions seemed almost trivial for his mind was in a state of near euphoria and he felt emotionally detached.

Jacky felt strange. He thought to himself, I have just been blown up and I ought to be in terrible agony, yet I feel so comfortable and relaxed. Jacky wondered briefly if he was dead and had gone to heaven. It seemed to be the only explanation of how he could have escaped so easily from such a terrible attack.

But he was not in heaven as he soon began to realize. He was actually floating in the air, just off the ground, and he was looking down on a severely injured body. The soldier was in a terrible state. He had lost one arm and there was blood everywhere. The soldier had obviously not been as lucky as Jacky.

Then the truth hit Jacky. The body down there was himself – he was the dead man who had been blown to pieces.

Surveying the scene with a curious detachment, Jacky watched as a US soldier arrived and checked whether the GI was dead, and then proceeded to rifle the body. He checked the pockets and then stripped off the boots.

Jacky could not understand why he did not feel angry at this man who was stealing his possessions. He ought to be yelling out and screaming that he was still alive, not dead. But from his vantage point, he merely observed the scene with curiosity, as more soldiers arrived and took what remained of him away in a body bag.

Only then did the truth hit him. They thought he was dead, and they were taking him away. But he was not dead. He was here, and was very close to them. Somehow, in some way he had survived. Yet none of his colleagues could see him. Why was this?

Then the darkness returned, and Jacky drifted off to sleep. When he awoke he was still floating at the peculiar angle just above his body. Only this time his battered body was laid out naked on a slab inside a large tented area. He recognized the area instantly as the temporary morgue at the nearby camp.

Standing by the body – his body – was the mortician. Jacky tried to cry out, to tell him that he was all right. But the man took no notice, he simply continued to fiddle with something in his hand – a syringe. He was testing it as if preparing to inject some liquid into the lifeless corpse.

Jacky felt a shift in his point of awareness. Suddenly he was no longer in the air above the body. He was back inside it. He felt overwhelming pain again as well as a terrible awareness of what was happening. He tried to speak, but no words would come out. But the movement he had made was enough. It alerted the mortician, who stood terrified, wide-eyed and uncomprehending for a few seconds. Then he screamed for help.

The mortician lay aside his syringe. The embalming fluid that he was just about to inject into Jacky's veins was no longer needed. Somehow, Jacky had come back to life.

A wounded US marine is dragged to safety during the Vietnam War. Jacky Bayne was not so lucky – he was hit by NVA rocket-fire and left for dead.

RETURN FROM DEATH · RETURN FROM DEATH · RETURN FROM DEATH · RETURN FROM RETURN FROM DEATH · RETURN FROM DEATH · RETURN FROM DEATH · RETURN FROM DEATH · RETURN FROM DEATH · RETURN FROM DEATH · RETURN FROM DEATH

Return from Death

Near-Death Experiences: The Doctor's Explanation

DR MICHAEL SABOM FROM GEORGIA took on the case in 1967 after Jacky Bayne had been discharged from the army and begun to make a slow recovery. He was stunned by the dramatic circumstances, but not entirely surprised. As a cardiologist he had often dealt with patients in a traumatic situation, where they had suffered a heart attack or undergone major surgery to repair blocked valves. More than once he had heard similar tales from them where they talked about floating out of their bodies and observing what was going on in a detached way. Often, he had realized, these incidents coincided with critical cases where the patient had almost died, but then pulled through and survived.

Sabom was sure there had to be a rational explanation for what happened. He talked with other doctors, many of whom had experienced similar incidents. The consensus among them was that at a point close to death the brain became starved of oxygen, and because of this hallucinations occurred. Mountaineers reported a feeling of light-headedness and euphoria when they climbed up to 7620m (25,000ft) where the air was very thin. They also said they sometimes saw strange things that were not really there.

But then there was a case that changed the Sabom's opinion. He was carefully monitoring the oxygen flow to the blood during an

Doctors knew of rare cases where too little anaesthetic was administered and the patient then claimed to be awake during surgery, experiencing all that was happening.

operation on one patient, as it was necessary to the complex surgical procedure. There were problems, but the patient survived and related an encounter that was similar to the other patients. He too had experienced a near-death vision. Yet Sabom had the medical proof that he was not suffering any lack of oxygen to the brain at the time that these events occurred. So the visions could not be explained that easily. There was also another possibility. Doctors knew of rare cases where too little anaesthetic was administered and the patient then claimed to be awake during surgery, experiencing all that was happening. Perhaps the person who was close to death overheard conversations in a semi-waking state of consciousness and they imagined that they were floating in the air?

However, Sabom again found a case that ruled out his theory. A woman described floating out of her body during an operation and going into another room in the hospital. Here she watched relatives who were debating

Floating out-of-body: patients have given accurate accounts of events around them whilst in comas.

her fate. The details that she related of the conversation were accurate, yet there was no way that this conversation could have been heard from the operating theatre. The only explanation seemed to be that the woman really had floated into the other room in an out-of-body state.

Sabom then asked patients who had suffered heart attacks but recalled no near-death encounter (NDE) to describe the scene that they presumed would have occurred during the attempts to revive them. As he expected, the information they gave was clearly just fantasy. But when he asked those people who claimed to have had a near-death, out-of-body experience, they gave astonishingly detailed descriptions of the equipment that was used to revive them.

From the way they related the information so accurately, it was obvious that they had not simply heard the medical staff talking through the procedure. It was as if the patients really had witnessed the operation and revival techniques that were used, even though it was medically impossible and sometimes physically impossible for them to have done so from the operating table. To see what they described they would need to have been floating in the air above their bodies – just as they claimed to have done.

The actual transition appeared to be far less taxing for the victim than it ever was for those left behind. In many ways it seemed almost to be a joyous occasion.

Life After Death: The Doctor's Story

DR ELISABETH KÜBLER-ROSS has cared for countless terminally ill patients during their final days. Her research has filled numerous volumes, such as the landmark work, *On Death and Dying,* which was published in 1969.

Dr Kübler-Ross noted a number of very interesting events during her research. The first thing was that death was never a traumatic experience. The actual transition appeared to be far less taxing for the victim than it ever was for those left behind. In many ways it seemed almost to be a joyous occasion. She cited numerous instances of patients whose faces lit up or who seemed positively to welcome death. Their fear dissipated and few people seemed to see it as anything other than a moment of release.

Moreover, many patients seemed far more aware of their imminent death than the medical staff. Sometimes they prepared themselves for one last visit from relatives and made it clear that this would be their last meeting. Although there was no reason why they should not survive for a few more days or weeks, they were normally correct in their judgement.

Dr Kübler-Ross also came upon a lot of cases where a person had unusual experiences at the point of death. She saw people who stared rapturously into empty space describing a light that they could see. Others talked animatedly with long-dead loved ones who seemed to be encouraging them to take that last step out of their body.

In conclusion, the doctor felt certain that death was not the terrible event that we imagine it to be. She came to believe we could learn from these experiences, and that possibly the process of death was merely a passage between different stages of life rather than the complete extinction of the body.

While Dr Kübler-Ross herself said that these many cases did not definitely prove life after death, she felt that they greatly increased the probability. She also noted some cases with direct links with the afterlife. In one case a dying woman seemed to be talking to a person in the afterlife and was informed that another relative was waiting to greet her. But this relative had died only recently, during the final stages of the woman's illness, and she had not been informed of the death deliberately. Yet she obviously felt they were going to be re-united, despite not knowing that this person had died.

Cases from Around the World: The Psychologist's Study

THE FIRST PERSON to collect NDEs was American psychologist Raymond Moody. His 1975 book entitled *Life After Life* became a huge bestseller. Moody had made no systematic attempt to study the cases he reported. He simply collected them from patients and told their stories in his book. But by bringing these tales together he had created a new field of study.

It was soon obvious that there had been reports of NDEs for centuries. But, as Moody's stories seemed to show, the NDEs were becoming more common during the

SWIMMING POOL DRAMA: A DROWNING MAN'S TALE

*I*N 1973 GEORGE CARPENTER appeared to die, but a few days later he managed to relate to me what had happened. George was swimming in a crowded public pool in Gloucestershire when he suddenly developed terrible cramps in his legs. He reports how he sank beneath the water like a stone.

'For a few moments I battled against the awful sensation of drowning. Then a strange calmness came over me. It no longer mattered whether I lived or died. My body was an object and my mind was not a part of it.'

As he descended into a curious, detached state of calmness all the sounds of the pool around him faded. He felt as if he were in a warm cocoon, and that his point of awareness had suddenly switched. Now he was outside the water, floating just above the pool, watching as the nearest people to him realized he was in difficulty and struggled to help him.

He watched their rescue efforts with dispassionate interest as if their success in reviving him did not really matter. George simply felt as if he was watching a drama on television. But he experienced neither pain nor any desperate urge to live. He was in fact distracted by what seemed to be a long tube or telescope that was pointing up into the sky. He felt himself rushing through the air towards it. At the end of the tube was a bright light that resembled hundreds of stars, and he was very eager to go through the tube and reach that light.

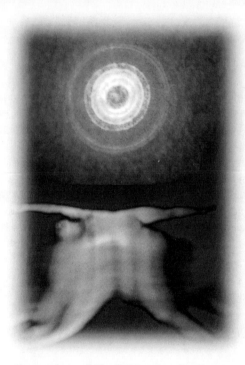

Racing toward the light: near-death cases all refer to a feeling of absolute peace.

George knew that once he passed into the tube and made it to the light there was no coming back. He simply knew that fact instinctively. But still he pressed on. As he did so there was an explosion of images in his mind, like a fantastic slide show being projected at great speed. Each was a scene from his life. He could even feel the emotions that were attached to those different times in his life.

Then he suddenly felt himself being pulled back. Before he knew it, he was opening his eyes back in his body and felt a searing pain as someone banged on his chest. Water was pumping out of his mouth and he could feel himself being dragged back to life. For some time he hated his rescuer. He had wanted to go on up towards that light, but gradually he saw how they had saved him from death.

Since George Carpenter told me of his near-fatal drowning, virtually identical stories have been told by thousands of people who have nearly died. An actor who was electrocuted on stage at Aviemore in Scotland by a faulty guitar watched a doctor rush from the audience and save him as he floated above, wanting to stay out of his body. A pilot driving home from an Oxfordshire airport lost control of his car and saw time slow right down as the vehicle crashed over an embankment. Then he floated out of his body, convinced that he was dead, but felt no pain until he was pulled back into his pain-racked body lying inside the twisted metal.

Near-death experiences, or NDEs as they came to be called, were soon recognized as the most common and potentially important phenomena to offer proof that there might be life after death.

second half of the twentieth century because medical techniques had improved so dramatically. In the past, many people who experienced an NDE would not have recovered. But now, with rapid responses to trauma and advanced emergency and casualty departments available in most countries, many victims of NDE were being saved quickly enough for them to recall what could so easily have been their last moments.

Moody went on to seek out cases of NDE from other cultures, rather than just the USA, to see if the phenomenon was the same or whether it differed according to local expectations. Generally the experience was the same all over the world. The out-of-body state, the light and the tunnel all seemed to be the same, as did the freedom from pain or feelings. There were rarer references to seeing dead relatives at the end of the passage. NDEs were also reported equally by religious or agnostic people. The near-death experience happened in about one in six cases of severe trauma. More people may have had an NDE, but simply could not remember it afterwards because their revival was followed immediately by long spells of unconsciousness or amnesia.

However, studies by Moody, and others later performed in a much more systematic fashion by University of Connecticut psychologist Dr Kenneth Ring, found an interesting new clue. When patients came back from death they were changed people. Often they took on a new spiritual lifestyle, had no fear of death, were keen to help others – even if they had previously been selfish – and had a great passion for the sanctity of life.

Generally the experience was the same all over the world. The out-of-body state, the light and the tunnel all seemed to be the same.

Dr Ring refined a sequence of events that progressed from being out of the body to reaching the end of the tube, tunnel, telescope or garden path (people used many different words to describe this phenomenon). It was found that most cases featured the early stages, such as the floating sensation and strange calmness, but few of them progressed all the way towards the light. Nobody went beyond that boundary. If they did, it seemed, they did not return. Many survivors of an NDE had instinctively felt that they faced a choice, either to move towards the light and die or return to life. It was not an easy decision to make.

There were some cultural differences. Those with a fervent religious belief sometimes said they saw God or Jesus in the light. Others merely spoke of 'wise beings' or

of seeing dead loved ones. The land beyond the tunnel was also somewhat tailored to individual impressions - a sunny garden was one of the common descriptions. The imagery of the NDE followed a set pattern but there were also individual variations.

The Man Who Did Not Die: The Climber's Tale

PETER LEE FROM LONDON was climbing a mountain in Germany with some friends when suddenly he felt the earth giving way beneath him and lost his footing. He crashed over the edge of a precipice heading towards what seemed a certain death. Lee relates how he fell down the mountainside, grasping at a clump of grass on the way – but his grip failed and he carried on falling down the cliff face.

As he fell, Lee recalls that his life flashed before his eyes. He says it was similar to film unwinding at great speed. This 'life review', while not reported widely during NDE cases, is cited in a substantial number of cases.

After these life images Peter Lee saw a tunnel opening up before his eyes. He says that he knew that this passageway meant the end of his current life but led to another one. As he was sucked into it he was also surrounded by people he recognized, some of whom were dead relatives and friends. Then he felt himself being pulled out of the tunnel, and he recalls thinking that he could not possibly be in heaven as his body was aching far too much.

Peter Lee had hit a snowdrift part of the way down the mountain and it had broken his fall. Although battered and bruised he was relatively unharmed, and had not even broken a single bone. That, of course, is the difference in this case. Although it has all the classic signs of an NDE this man was never physically near to death. He obviously believed that he was, but in the end he had a lucky escape.

Do such cases suggest that it is possible to have an NDE simply by fearing that death is imminent? This presumably can be interpreted to mean that the NDE is not just a physical phenomenon, but something that occurs primarily at the level of human consciousness.

The Dying Brain Theory: A Psychologist's Deliberations

CASES LIKE THAT REPORTED by Peter Lee are considered very important to the psychologist Dr Sue Blackmore who works at the University of the West of England. She believes that his story helps to show that the NDE that results from well understood changes within the brain at a point where it believes that it is close to death.

Blackmore argues that the NDE results from a combination of different events that occur inside the brain. When danger is perceived natural hormones, known as endorphins, are released. These dull any bodily pain and create a state of euphoria. There is plenty of medical evidence for these hormones being released when there is a crisis and could well be the reason why NDE witnesses talk of their calm state of mind.

But what of the ability of someone to drift out of their body and look down on themselves from mid-air? This, Dr Blackmore contends, results from a breakdown of the normal functions of the brain as it is starved of oxygen. As it struggles to regain some order it creates an image of the person it believes itself to be. While this idea has some merit, it also has presents a multitude of problems. Why does the person create an image of themselves where they are very clearly still in the place of danger? Why do they not imagine themselves on a desert island or safe in their own homes?

As for rationalizing the tunnel of light, Blackmore has run computer simulations based on random firing of brain cells as they start to break down. She claims the resulting image can look like a tunnel and the mind simply translates these physical symptoms into the imagery of a tube, or telescope.

The reports of meetings with dead relatives, or the question of whether to return to life or remain in the pain-free afterlife, are seen by the psychologist as a consequence of the brain's ongoing battle for survival.

Undoubtedly, some aspects of this dying brain theory work well, such as the explanations for the sense of calm and possibly the origin of the tunnel image. But it does not really give an explanation for the unusual aspects of the NDE – the out-of-the-body experience, encounters with dead relatives, and the sense of heading towards something wonderful.

Dr Blackmore fights back by noting that the worldwide consistencies between the reports do occur not because the event is real, but because all human beings have brains that live (and die) in the same way.

Children's Stories: A Doctor's Research

THE RESEARCH OF SEATTLE doctor, Melvin Morse, makes a unique contribution to the NDE debate, for he has concentrated on reports of the NDE made by young children. He has met many in his specialist paediatric care of seriously ill and dying children. To his surprise Dr Morse discovered that these children, who were often only two or three years old, report near-death experiences identical to those of adults. This is unexpected, because one of the most common arguments of the sceptic is that the person having a near-death vision is at least to some degree seeing what they expect to see. The images will, of course, be based on years of indoctrination about death and the afterlife. But children of this age do not yet even understand what death is, let alone have views about what happens when you die.

Morse has numerous drawings made by children in which they graphically portray the ability to see themselves from above their own bodies, tunnels, lights at the end and the beautiful place to which they believe they were heading before being brought back to life.

It is difficult to hear case histories without suspecting that some

Dr Sue Blackmore's illustration of the 'tunnel' – a common feature in near-death case studies.

fundamentally real experience must be behind them. One four-year-old child born with a heart defect is a typical example of the innocence involved in some of these cases. I discovered his story when I shared a hospital ward in Birkenhead with his mother. When he was old enough to be operated upon, surgeons had decided to replace a faulty valve in his heart with a plastic one.

Naturally, he was too young to be told what was happening, or why. But when he came to after surgery the first thing he said was: 'Mummy, why wouldn't the doctors speak to me when I was floating up by the ceiling?' He described in detail how during the operation he had found himself outside his body watching the procedure in the theatre and seeing them place the valve inside his body on the table below. He was able to describe the valve, although he had never seen an artificial heart valve before.

The Hunt for Proof: Other Reports

DR SUE BLACKMORE HAS commented that she would be willing to review her dying brain theory if there were NDE cases where a person clearly saw something that they could not have seen unless they were really out of their bodies.

Melvin Morse has a case that seems to fit the proof required by Dr Blackmore. A woman in a hospital room in Seattle was narrowly saved from death by an emergency resuscitation team. When she recovered she described a near-death experience in which she had floated in the corner of the room at the top of a window and looked down on her body. When the medical team were disinclined to believe her, she insisted that she could prove it because of a tennis shoe that was on the ledge outside the building.

The staff looked out of the window, but could not see any shoe. The woman insisted that you could not see it from that angle and that you had to be higher up, just as she had been during her NDE. One of the staff members went outside and looked. Sure enough, there was a tennis shoe, exactly as the woman claimed. It was brought into the room and she was asked to describe it before it was revealed. The woman did so exactly.

To try and establish proof once and for all a remarkable experiment has been set up by Dr Peter Fenwick, a neurophysiologist from the Maudsley Hospital in London. A number of symbols have been secretly placed on the ceilings of various emergency rooms and operating theatres at hospitals around Britain. Even the hospital staff have not been informed of what or where they are. The aim of this experiment is to collate NDE reports from patients revived in these locations and see whether they claim to have seen these marks, which are impossible to be seen from below.

Dr Fenwick refuses to discuss the results gathered so far, as this is a programme set to run for several years, but he says that the evidence from NDEs is potentially very persuasive. Perhaps, thanks to his efforts, it may soon be rather more substantial than that.

So What Did Happen?

You now have the evidence to decide what happened to American GI Jacky Bayne after he was struck by mortars and rockets during the Vietnam war.

● *Was his experience of seeing himself from outside his body a result of the stress that he was under and simply an hallucination? Perhaps in a semi-conscious state he had a dream where he saw the other soldiers talking over his body, presuming that he was dead.*

● *Alternatively, as Dr Sue Blackmore contends, did the whole experience result from what she calls the dying brain theory? Was Jacky so close to death that his brain cells started to disintegrate because the flow of oxygen was restricted? This in turn could have caused him to suffer from a false sense of reality. His lack of pain and calm state of mind could have been the result of the natural endorphins being pumped through his bloodstream after the trauma of the attack. Or is he truly describing what happened, but misinterpreting normal physical processes for a mystical experience?*

● *The third possibility is that Jacky Bayne really came close to the point of physical death and his mind somehow separated from his body and floated free, hovering in an unknown hinterland between life and death. He could just have been experiencing what we will all one day encounter when we die. So does it prove that there is some other stage of existence beyond life on earth?*

MONSTER FROM THE DEEP · MONSTER FROM THE DEEP · MONSTER FROM
MONSTER FROM THE DEEP · MONSTER FROM THE DEEP · MON-
MONSTER FROM THE DEEP · MONSTER FROM THE DEEP · MONSTER FROM THE
MONSTER FROM THE DEEP · MONSTER FROM THE DEEP
MONSTER FROM THE DEEP · MONSTER FROM THE DEEP · MONSTER FROM THE DEEP
MONSTER FROM THE DEEP · MONSTER FROM THE DEEP · MONSTER FROM

CASE STUDY

Monster from the Deep

The Monster from the Deep

THE CREATURE FIRST APPEARED on 8 January 1998 and nobody knew what it was. Within moments of its discovery, the local folk who lived near Four Mile Beach in Tasmania were talking animatedly of sea monsters. Before the day was out the news was to travel around the world. At last there was some definitive proof that water monsters were real because a body had been found.

The day had begun quietly enough for the fishermen on this usually sleepy beach. But that peace was shattered when they found something extraordinary that had been washed up by the tide. It was as if a crack had opened up between our world and some other reality and left an alien being on our planet.

The dead creature on the beach gave off a bad, fishy odour. Nobody knew what it was. Even those who had fished the local waters for decades had never seen anything like it. Rumours about monsters and invasions from aliens were rife in the local community.

The 'blobster', as some began to call it, was something like a cross between a giant octopus and a hairy cow pat. It was enormous – at least 6m (20ft) long. Yet all that was washed up on the beach was a rotting carcass that was covered in sand and a mass of shaggy hair. This suggested that its original size may have been even larger. Its oval mass was surrounded by what appeared to be many short tentacles or legs that clung to the beach. Nobody could move it because the creature was very heavy indeed.

Arguments about what it might be began immediately. It was clearly too big to be any of the obvious marine life in the area, such as a dolphin, even if one was so badly mutilated after death. When all the major marine life had been eliminated from the discussion, it was then broached that the creature was a sea monster of the type that used to be reported in apocryphal tales from ancient mariners. More recently these huge dinosaur-like creatures are reported to have moved to the many large lakes that were once fed by the sea. Several of these are situated in the northern hemisphere. These rarely seen creatures are often given pet names by the locals, and tourist industries grow up around them.

But science was never convinced by eyewitness evidence that was unsupported. For scientists demanded physical proof of these creatures before they accepted something that defied their views of the natural world. If monsters lived in the water, they argued, then they also died in the water. Sooner or later one or two of those unknown beasts would have to be washed ashore by freak tides or other conditions. But in several hundreds of years this had not happened. Where were the bodies, they demanded?

Now, on this lonely beach on an island off the south coast of Australia, it seemed as if the scientists' demands had finally been met. Here was the proof that had long been sought. A completely new species had been found that was the type of creature that so many people had claimed to have witnessed across the centuries.

The 6 m (20 ft) long 'blobster' that washed up on the shores of Tasmania's Four Mile Beach in January 1988.

Bodies of Evidence: Different Accounts

THE TASMANIAN 'BLOBSTER' was, surprisingly enough, not unique. Records from those who pursue zoological anomalies note half a dozen similar discoveries. One of the strangest happened in 1808, when a massive creature 17m (55ft) long was found on the beach on Stronsay Island in the Orkneys. Witnesses who saw it described the creature as having a long neck, humped tail and legs that resembled flippers. It was remarkably like the lake monsters, one of which was to be seen later at Loch Ness. Unfortunately, the violent storm that had washed up the creature battered it against rocks and then took the remains back to the ocean before any scientists could reach the area.

Another creature was found on a Tasmanian beach in July 1960. Unfortunately, the scientific researchers were very slow to react to the decomposing corpse, and unbelievably it was 1962 before any material was flown to Hobart to be studied. No definite conclusion was then reached on what type of creature it was, and the experts disagreed on their opinions, but most of them felt that the gooey mess that was left was simply blubber that had been stripped from a dead whale.

However, the most intriguing case of all occurred off the New Zealand coast on 25 April 1977 when the Japanese trawler the *Zuiyo Maru* caught a 'monster' by accident in its nets. This strange creature was hauled

The long-necked creature hooked by the Zuiyo Maru *in 1977.*

aboard the boat by ropes. It was then suspended over the deck, where it was photographed. The creature had not completely rotted as had the previous finds on beaches. This one was a long-necked, humped monster, 10m (33ft) long, and was obviously not a decaying shark. Indeed sharks of such a large size are very rare.

After taking the photographs, Captain Tanaka bowed to pressure from his crew, along with his own fears that his catch would be contaminated by the foul smelling beast. The monster was put back in the sea. But fibres were taken from the creature so that they could be assessed along with the photographs back at Tokyo University. When tests were done a chemical that was common to sharks was traced. So it appeared as if it might well have been a giant shark after all, the flesh of which had stripped away from the body during decomposition creating the monster-like appearance.

Then in 1992 nanny Louise Whipps, who was on holiday at Benbecula in the Scottish Hebrides, found what seemed to be a smaller cousin of the Tasmanian blobster. This was only 3.6m (12ft) long, but it had the same oval body with short fins and a curved tail. Louise's photograph of herself sitting by the foul smelling corpse was unseen by experts and just kept as a family curiosity until 1996 when she handed it to the Hancock Museum in Newcastle-upon-Tyne. They put the picture on display asking marine biologists and zoologists to help solve the mystery for them. Nobody ever came forward, but with the discovery of the larger and very similar Tasmanian creature in 1998 there seems little doubt that the two creatures are of the same species.

Oliver Crimmen, sea-life expert at the Natural History Museum, considered the options for what this beast might be. When a shark body rots, the gills leave pieces of flesh that resemble tentacles. But the lack of any backbone in the remains of either creature did not support this theory. Could the remains just be whale blubber as in the Tasmania find in 1960? If so, the formation of the many

tentacles would be a fluke and unlikely to happen twice in six years. It was not a squid or an octopus. Nobody knew what the creature was.

However, once again, tests on the samples of the Tasmanian creature pointed towards it being a decayed shark with the appropriate DNA. So did this mean that water monsters did not really exist?

Submarine Life: Local legends

THERE HAVE BEEN REPORTS of a strange creature in Loch Ness in Scotland for well over a thousand years. Until the 1920s this 'inland sea' was almost inaccessible. Unless you lived in one of the villages scattered around the loch you were unlikely to visit the area. But then a new road that went round the lake for several miles was opened. As a result tourists were attracted there, which also coincided with the first flood of what is now an annual batch of monster reports.

Was it a coincidence or as some cynics suggest, was the old legend given a helping hand by locals who saw the chance to attract visitors to their isolated area? Certainly the first two photographs of the monster, taken soon after the new road opened, are probably not of any strange creature, even though to this day locals say they are.

A photograph that was taken at Foyers on 12 November 1933 seems to show a

Robert Wilson's 1934 shot of the Loch Ness monster – a picture that fooled the world for 59 years.

'thrashing monster' that resembles a snake on the churned-up water surface. Or, at least, it does until you look at it again and see it as an out-of-focus shot of a dog with a stick in its mouth swimming towards you. Then it seems very unconvincing. Nobody has established that this picture is a deliberate hoax, but at best it is unpersuasive evidence.

Only months later, on 19 April 1934, surgeon Robert Wilson took the first major photograph of 'Nessie' as the creature was nicknamed. This photograph, taken at the loch at Invermoriston and (when shown full frame) featuring the far shore in the background, shows an animal with a long neck and head above water, surrounded by ripples. It certainly looks impressive. The media championed the photograph and it was seen around the world. Unfortunately, again, it was always a source of some doubt to researchers. These doubts soon grew as more sophisticated photographic analysis became available.

The 'surgeon's photo', as it is usually called, has one big flaw. The scale just does not seem right. The size of the ripples and the distance to the far shore do not suggest that this is a large creature. Of course, books, magazines and TV shows often do not reproduce the full image. They show only a blow-up of the monster itself, with no shoreline, so it can seem more genuine (see below).

Research by serious experts led to speculation that this famous photograph was of an otter frozen by the camera in an accidental pose that made it seem like a monster. Then tests revealed that, whatever the creature was, it could not have been much bigger than about 30cm (1ft). So it was hardly the frightening beast of legendary fame!

Finally, in 1992 the truth was slowly revealed. Lambert Wilson (no relation to the photographer),

Dr Robert Rines, pictured during his search for the Loch Ness monster in the 1970s.

who was 86, claimed that he was the monster. He alleged that he had swum under water holding up a monster head from a toy shop and allowed himself to be photographed.

Two years later, David Martin, a zoologist who worked as part of a science team that investigated the loch, uncovered more details. A notorious local hoaxer, so it appeared, had created the model using a toy submarine. Martin and a colleague suggested that the surgeon was involved in the prank, but all were unprepared for the publicity the photograph got and could not then reveal that it was a fake. Lambert Wilson, on the other hand, says the surgeon was an innocent by-stander. Either way the most famous photograph of the Loch Ness monster appears to have no credibility.

Underwater Pictures: The Academy's Researches

BETWEEN 1972 AND 1975 the Academy of Applied Sciences in Boston decided to visit Scotland to try to solve the riddle of the Loch Ness monster. Dr Robert Rines was leader of the expedition.

The initial visit was unexpectedly successful. Using underwater cameras to peer through the peat-filled waters near Urquhart Castle, scene of many of the best sightings, some remarkable images were obtained. They were matched with sonar readings at the same time that indicated that a large object was in the water at the spot where the photographs were taken.

Some time later the photographs were shown to the world. They were fuzzy and dim because the water was so murky. But what could have been a diamond-shaped flipper was indeed visible in close-up. They were the most intriguing images of the monster.

These pictures were again shown all over the world and led to much speculation about whether the monster really did exist. There were some surprising converts. Naturalist Sir Peter Scott told journalists that he had a very appropriate name for the creature that described its diamond-like fin – *Nessiterras rhombopteryx*. It was some

> *With enhancement a grotesque head and neck of what appeared to be a classic monster emerged from the dark waters.*

time before people realized that this was in fact an anagram for 'monster hoax by Sir Peter S'.

Of course, Scott had hoaxed nobody, but his jovial caution was justified. The second Rines expedition revealed even more amazing photographs that were taken underwater near the castle. The murky shots had to be processed by computer to show anything at all, which was a point that was not often appreciated by those who viewed the shots. With enhancement a grotesque head and neck of what appeared to be a classic monster emerged from the dark waters.

However, far from being seen as definitive proof, this new evidence ended up being the undoing of the honourable efforts by the Boston academy. For this monster looked rather too familiar to some people. This was because in 1969 a film called *The Private Lives of Sherlock Holmes* was shot at Loch Ness. For the film a life-sized model of the monster was used. After the shooting ended the plastic beast was sunk beneath the waters off Urquhart Castle – in the same area, in fact, where the Rines team found their evidence.

This was to prove to be an abject lesson to all scientists who sought to find an answer to the mysterious monster from the deep. Even when the evidence appears to be decisive, it needs to be thoroughly checked for flaws.

Different Sightings: The Monster-Hunters' Stories

DESPITE THE SERIOUS PROBLEMS of the early evidence in connection with the Loch Ness monster, there are good pieces of data that encourage hunters of the creature to camp out by the lake each summer. These include naturalists such as Adrian Shine, who thinks that the animal is real but may only be some kind of mutant fish. Much data is recorded by the Loch Ness Investigation Bureau, which gets involved in its own and other more organized research efforts each year. Some of the more recent investigations have been quite strange. These include scouring the loch in a yellow submarine and trying to find different lures to attract the monster to the surface.

One of the most interesting researches was Operation Deepscan in 1987, where a flotilla of small boats trailed sonar equipment up and down the surface area to map the water. For several days they found nothing and the media went home disappointed. Then on the very last day they picked up a large moving object that they were unable to explain. Unfortunately, nothing could be seen of this object as it was deep under water.

In July 1992 Project Urquhart utilized a well equipped scientific vessel to conduct a marine life survey of the loch. On 27 July they succeeded in tracking a large and solid target too big for any fish as it moved from Foyers to Invermoriston. Such recent expeditions inspired a 1995 film called *Loch Ness*, starring Ted Danson as a sceptical American researcher whose sonar scan of the loch changes his views forever.

A month later, on 15 August 1992, the first known camcorder footage of what might be the monster was recorded near Urquhart Castle. Little more than a churning of water is visible, as something moves across the surface. Adrian Shine compares it to a 'cycling motion' and wonders if it is just a wave. Others, such as zoologist Peter Meadows, were more intrigued and were amazed by the recorded images.

1996 proved to be another interesting year at the loch. It began with a camcorder film taken at Invermoriston at lunch time on 5 August. It records for two minutes the passage of a distant undulating set of dark humps just breaking the surface. Ian Finlayson, his wife Vera, their son and his friend were picnicking at the time and all saw the creature, but Vera suspected that it was just a giant eel.

A few days later, again at Invermoriston, retired soldier Frank Wilson was teaching the two sons of a local friend to fish when they heard a big 'wooshing' sound. They then observed a large object that was just below the surface moving past their range of vision about 91.5m (300ft) out. Only the top of a flipper was visible before the object submerged, but they could tell that the animal was at least 9m (30ft) long. Wilson managed to take several photographs.

And so the stories continue. Yet another ex-soldier, Richard White, was driving to Foyers on 21 March 1997 when he saw a disturbance in the water across the loch

Sonar soundings being taken of Loch Ness during 1987's Operation Deepscan – a search for definitive proof of the Loch Ness Monster.

near Urquhart Castle. As he stopped to observe this curious sight two tourists in a car did the same. White retrieved his camera and took some shots of a small head or neck sticking out of the water. It does not appear at all large but it was enough to win him the £500 William Hill prize that was awarded in early 1998 in recognition of the best visual evidence for the monster for the preceding year. Bookmakers William Hill now offer odds of just 250 to 1 that physical proof of Nessie will arrive before the end of 1999.

Natural Phenomena: The Sceptic's Opinion

STEUART CAMPBELL IS A FASCINATING character. He is an architect by trade, lives in Edinburgh, and has a passion for finding rational answers to seemingly supernatural matters. He writes for the sceptical media about his determined quest to resolve unusual cases. As a fervent Scottish nationalist he is fiercely protective of Scotland's heritage, but does not wish to see it usurped by outsiders who are just trying to get famous or to make money.

Campbell has investigated much of the evidence about the Loch Ness monster and finds it lacking in substance. In his opinion, what happens inside the Loch is a combination of ordinary events that can appear to be mysterious.

He notes that there are natural phenomena that can look like monsters. For example, the surface of Loch Ness can behave strangely and allow standing waves to travel across the surface many minutes after any boat that initially caused them has left the area. Such freak waves can resemble a creature swimming just below the surface of the water. And in fact nearly all of the monster photographs show little more than disturbances to the surface water some distance away from the witness.

Another problem is that there is much rotting vegetation below the water's surface, including tree trunks that have fallen into the loch. When the trunks decay they can release gases which can make the log rise back up to the surface for a time. Seen from a distant shore this might easily fool someone into thinking that a monster has just surfaced from the loch.

Campbell has investigated much of the evidence about the Loch Ness monster and finds it lacking in substance . . . a combination of ordinary events that can appear to be mysterious

There is also a considerable amount of wildlife that can appear deceptive from a distance. These include otters diving into the water and unusually large fish or eels. All of these creatures actually live in the loch.

Campbell also believes that a number of hoaxes have been carried out over the years. He has exposed some dubious photographs and made some very critical comments about some of the better known photographers. These include Frank Searle or magician 'Doc' Shiels, who even says that he has evoked monsters using ceremonies featuring nubile young women.

Although these people deny trickery, it is undoubtedly true that some of the best visual evidence has turned out upon investigation to be the least reliable. The evidence that remains from still photos and camcorder images rarely show much more than wakes trailing across the surface, or a very slight disturbance in the water. Unfortunately, these are cases where many possible explanations exist as to what may have been filmed. As such, the recorded images from Loch Ness are not as spectacular as they might first appear.

Lake Monsters: Tales from North America

LOCH NESS IS BY NO MEANS the only place where lake monsters have been sighted. Indeed, there are few large inland lakes in the world that do not have some stories associated with them.

On the border between Canada and the USA there are vast chains of lakes and many of them feature their own monster. Mark Chorvinsky from Rockville, Maryland, has set up a monster database to try to keep track of them all.

Two of the most sighted monsters have been given names and legends have built up around them. But sightings of these creatures date back almost as far as those for Nessie. Lake Champlain's first report of a serpent-like creature was recorded in 1609 when the French explorer Samuel de Champlain was the first European to discover the spectacular location. This is a very scenic ribbon lake on the border between Quebec and Vermont, that is 169 km (105 miles) long by 19 km (12 miles) wide. The creature, nicknamed Champ, has been seen often over the years.

THE PREVIOUS LIFE · THE PREVIOUS LIFE · THE PREVIOUS LIFE · THE PREVIOUS
PREVIOUS LIFE · THE PREVIOUS LIFE · THE PREVIOUS LIFE · THE
THE PREVIOUS LIFE · THE PREVIOUS LIFE · THE PREVIOUS LIFE
LIFE · THE PREVIOUS LIFE · THE PREVIOUS LIFE · PREVI-
PREVIOUS LIFE · THE PREVIOUS LIFE · THE PREVIOUS LIFE
IOUS LIFE · THE PREVIOUS LIFE · THE PREVIOUS LIFE · THE PREVIOUS

CASE STUDY

The Previous Life

LAKE ELSINORE IS A PRETTY little spa town in the mountains south of the urban sprawl that is Los Angeles. The Californian sunshine makes it a perfect spot to take a weekend break. Maureen Williamson had lived in the area since 1970, and by the autumn of 1986 she had a regular group of friends that she would meet in the local coffee shop. They met as usual in November, and Maureen ordered some carrot cake, which her friends thought was very odd as she did not like carrot cake. But then something even more puzzling happened. Maureen started to scribble on the table, and before she knew it she had written the words 'John Daniel Ashford'.

All her friends asked her who the man was. Jokingly they asked if he was her lover. 'Certainly not', Maureen replied. She was obviously as confused as they were. She had no idea who the man might be, and had never heard the name before.

At the time Maureen was seeing a local therapist, Dr Marge Rieder, who was trying to help with some painful memories and bad dreams that were giving her night-mares. To investigate these problems the doctor had been using relaxation therapy and hypnotic regression, gently coaxing Maureen back to her childhood in the hope that this would help to overcome her hidden fears. This technique is often successfully used by psychotherapists.

When Maureen told her doctor about buying the carrot cake and then writing the man's name, they both assumed that the person must be someone from her past that she had consciously forgotten. Perhaps the stranger was a part of her painful memories and his identity had come through from her subconscious as a result of her therapy. So Marge Rieder took her patient back under hypnosis to her earliest days and asked the question: 'Who is John Daniel Ashford?' Neither woman was to be prepared for the reply that came.

'He is my husband', Maureen asserted in her hypnotic state as if it were the most obvious thing in the world.

But her doctor knew that this was impossible as Maureen had not been married before. Events then got even more confused. Maureen insisted that she lived in a town called Marlborough in the state of Virginia. She also said that her name was Becky and that the year was 1861.

Gradually the story of Becky and John Ashford evolved over a series of hypnosis sessions over the next few months. She gave a very detailed account of how she was born in Herndon in 1835, and grew up as a tomboy. At the age of 13 she met a man called John Daniel Aushlick, but she always called him Ashford as it was easier to pronounce. Despite her young age they moved to Marlborough and got married. However, Becky and John were not destined to have a happy life for the American Civil War intervened. Virginia was in the South, and acted as a railway supply route, particularly for horses. Becky befriended and then began an affair with a Northern soldier called Charley, who had been wounded at the Battle of Shiloh and had switched sides to become a spy for the Confederacy.

By reliving her own death at the hands of this assassin, many of Maureen Williamson's nightmares then ceased. It seemed as if her memories had not come from her traumatic childhood, as had been assumed, but from a previous life where she had lived and died as someone else.

Becky's husband John had been raised in an Indian camp at Robin's Nest. His name had previously been Pony Boy, as he had an Indian father and a European immigrant mother, who smuggled him into Marlborough soon after birth. However, John's upbringing had left him sympathetic to the anti-slavery laws of the North, and he sought to end the spying activities of Becky's lover without even being aware of their secret affair. A local villain, sent by John to silence Charley, was also unaware that the woman this spy was seeing was really the wife of John Ashford. As a result, and because of the ongoing war, he took revenge on Charley by taking Becky aside and strangling her to death in full view of one of her children.

By reliving her own death at the hands of this assassin, many of Maureen Williamson's nightmares then ceased. It seemed as if her memories had not come from her traumatic childhood, as had been assumed, but from a previous life where she had lived and died as someone else.

Yet still this amazing story was not over, for during the course of the next seven years it became apparent that many of the people who had lived in Marlborough in the 1860s were once again living together as a community in and around Lake Elsinore during the 1990s.

Maureen (while hypnotised and living as Becky) recognized one woman in the community as having once been John's mother. By 1995 over 50 different people, some of whom were already friends, others who were not acquainted in their present life, were all regressed by Dr Rieder and each relived a life in that Virginian town a century earlier. Their stories seemed to match and a remarkable tale evolved. It consisted mainly of the people relating mostly mundane activities in the local shops and school of what was a relatively unknown town.

Most of the people who told these stories had no other recollection of this past life. A few, like Maureen, had experienced dreams of places and people they did not recognize, or had unusual yearnings for foods that they did not normally like. The carrot cake, in fact, had been a favourite of John Ashford's – a treat that Becky had baked for him often. Only a few who were identified by others as having lived in this previous time were reluctant to be regressed, and new members of this extraordinary past-life community continue to be recognized even to this day.

Of course, many people suspected a gigantic hoax. Had these Californian people got together and created this story just for fun, or to make some money from the case's attendant publicity? But the participants denied this. For some it was such a shocking revelation that they just wanted to forget all about it, to reinter the memories that had surfaced. But for others it was an incredible discovery that served to change their lives. They were then determined to find more information that would prove their story was true and that reincarnation really exists.

Millboro, Virginia was the site of a railhead during the American Civil War.

EVIDENCE

The Previous Life

In Search of the Past: Finding the Links

WHEN MAUREEN WILLIAMSON first made the claim that she was once called Becky Aushlick (Ashford) and lived in Marlborough, the search began in earnest to establish whether any of this could actually be true. But there was an immediate problem. While there was, indeed, a Herndon in Virginia, there was no place called Marlborough. However, there was a town called Millboro, and it seemed to be situated in the correct area.

This small place was not well known for its association with the Civil War, but it had indeed possessed a railhead, as described by the hypnotised gathering. There was no published source that appeared to describe the details of Civil War life in this backwater. But it was learned that Millboro had at the time been spelt as Millborough, which was even closer to the pronunciation that Maureen had used. Also, many of the people who had been regressed used terms that seemed out of place in 20th-century America. Becky spoke of using a nappy on her baby, a British word, whereas Americans normally use the word diaper. The locals in Millboro, when talking under hypnosis, also referred to bonfires on Guy Fawkes Day, which is a British celebration not familiar to many Americans.

Millboro was in Bath County and was part of an area settled by many people who came from the west of England. In the 1860s most of the residents were still close to their homeland and only one or two generations removed, so they would still have been familiar with their British heritage.

Although some details were found that matched the stories, such as place names, possible buildings and traces of the Aushlick family (although no John Aushlick), the true test had to be to visit the present-day town. So some of the participants in this unusual story, with Maureen amongst them, went with Dr Rieder to see if they could recognize anything in the town in the present day. No one had ever visited the state before – at least in this lifetime.

Many of the people who had been regressed used terms that seemed out of place in 20th-century America.

The trip proved to be a fascinating exercise. They did indeed claim to locate certain buildings and pointed out places of long-gone landmarks, even when new buildings were now located on the sites. On the other hand, there was no trace in the available historical records of the tragic death of Becky or the spying activities of her lover, which seems very strange. Maureen wondered if the townsfolk had covered up these nasty events because of the war and the shameful nature of what happened.

Unfortunately, most of the town's records had been destroyed in a fire 90 years before, making any real proof hard to find. And searches through other sources of possible evidence were just as fruitless. Yet there was one very interesting discovery. Despite quickly recognizing that there was no Marlborough and that the town of Millboro had to be the correct location, Maureen Williamson continued to insist on the previous name whenever reliving her past life. The visit to Millboro revealed that the name probably had derived from Marlborough in England's West Country and that Millborough (and even today's Millboro) was spoken by the locals in such a way that it sounded very like the name that Maureen had phonetically said under hypnosis. That someone should know this without having lived in the area in the present day, let alone having ever visited it, did seem to be quite remarkable.

Past Lives: Historical Evidence

THERE IS A PROBLEM WITH cases of alleged past lives. This revolves around the discovery of documentation to back up the details. If there are no records of the people involved in a supposed series of events in the past, the reality of the case cannot be proven. If, on the other hand, such records are found and are easily accessible then those who are sceptical can rightly suggest that they were the source of an invented story.

Even when witnesses insist that they did not fabricate a past-life account, there are still further reasons to doubt their story. This stems from a discovery made by American brain surgeon, Dr Wilder Penfield, when operating on patients during the 1950s. Because there are no pain receptors in the brain, surgery can be done while the patient is conscious. When certain parts of the brain were stimulated by electrical charges, patients reported memories flooding back in dramatic flashbacks, often with all the senses intact. The memories came from long-forgotten incidents. It was soon realized that the brain appears capable of storing fantastic amounts of information, possibly even all the sensory impressions that a person has experienced. Only rarely do these surface into consciousness. This process is known as cryptomnesia.

The importance of this research to past-life memories cannot be overstated. It means that a person may truthfully assert that they had never heard of or read about a town called Millboro during the Civil War but that they could have been told about the place, possibly as a child, or they might even have heard a conversation while in their cot. Years later those memories could possibly resurface and be unconsciously moulded into a past life.

That this can happen, especially when altered states of consciousness such as hypnotic regression are involved, is now without doubt. This was first clearly established by a case involving a woman who was regressed by Welsh therapist Arnold Bloxham to two past lives. One life was as a tutor's wife who served the Roman emperor in AD 286 and the other was a Jewess who was killed in a massacre at York in 1190. Melvin Harris, a researcher who was sceptical of past-life memories, spent much time researching the evidence for this case, and came to a damning conclusion.

In the story of the York Jewess it was found that much of the story relied upon modern misconceptions rather than historical fact, such as refer-ring to Coppergate as having copper gates, when in fact the name derived from Cooper's Gate. The saga of Livonia, the Roman woman, was even more significant. Harris found two novels by Louis de Wohl that had all the same characters and plots in them and were set in the same time period. Although some of the characters were historically real, Livonia was one of those invented by the author. While there was no evidence that the regressed

woman could recall ever readings these novels, or indeed about the events in York in 1190, the latter were well documented and both novels were in print long before her hypnosis. The likelihood seems strong that she had come across this material, forgotten all about it, and then through cryptomnesia it had become the basis of a past life story told under hypnosis.

Of course, as Harris and others have argued since, if this process can be fortuitously established in this particular case, how frequently does it happen when we never find the source?

Invented or Real?: A hypnotist's findings

ONE MAN WHO IS WELL placed to judge past-life cases is hypnotherapist Joe Keeton from the Wirral in Britain. He has probably regressed more people to alleged past lives than anyone else in Britain and, quite possibly, anyone in the world. He has worked with hundreds of such people.

Keeton argues that many people cannot reach the correct level of hypnosis to successfully come up with a past life. But once they can get to that state, subsequent regressions are relatively easy. However, it is rare for only one past life to be related. Most people are able to report a whole series of them. Usually these are from lives where they were the same sex as their present incarnation, but sometimes there are exceptions. In these exceptions, amongst a typical recall of six past lives, one of them will most likely have lived a life as a person of the opposite sex.

This is actually very interesting, because if each person lives past lives as a mixture of sexes there should be at least a proportion who today are in the 'minority' sex for the soul of that individual. Those people should therefore have a recall of past lives that would be mostly of a different sex from their present one. If past lives are somehow being invented or imagined then the chances are that the majority of people would would choose to create past lives that fit with their present sex. This is what appears to emerge from the evidence, so is this significant?

> *Because there are no pain receptors in the brain, surgery can be done while the patient is conscious. When parts of the brain were stimulated by electrical charges, patients reported memories flooding back in dramatic flashbacks.*

Hypnotherapist Joe Keeton, who, through his regression therapy techniques, has come across hundreds of cases of past-life memories.

Keeton also reports that while cryptomnesia may have a part to play, many of the past lives found during his studies are of very ordinary existences. Not only are these most unlikely to have been recorded in any published source to act as a spur for cryptomnesia, but they do not have the expected excitement that would be found in someone making up a past-life account. Contrary to what most people assume, past lives are rarely action-filled adventures as exotic pharaohs or princesses. People never seem to recall a life as a celebrated historical character, Keeton's only exception being someone who lived a life as Nell Gwynne. Generally, in the many existences that are related, people live ordinary lives and suffer sickness and often die in poverty. A person is far more likely to recall a poor life tending pigs on a rural farm than to report a grand existence as a wealthy character in opulent surroundings.

Another touch of realism from these cases was discovered in Keeton's work. Although he is himself unsure as to what the explanation for these cases must be, he notes that if the past life goes much further back in time than 400 years it becomes more difficult to communicate with the person who is under hypnosis. It is as if they simply do not recognize the language and terms that are being used.

Of course, that would be the case if you were to suddenly find yourself talking to someone from the Middle Ages. To them, you would be speaking a foreign language. But if these stories were nothing but inventions, Keeton points out, most people would be unaware of this fact because historical movies and TV plays always depict people in the past speaking modern English. They would therefore have no problem understanding their hypnotist.

Fascinating Accounts: A Soldier's Story

A CASE THAT ILLUSTRATES the problems faced when one attempts to investigate past lives is that of a Berkshire man, Ray Bryant. In a series of past lives brought out over several years by Joe Keeton (some sessions of which I recorded on tape), he has been everything from a girl who died as a child to a drunken coachman. If he is acting, either consciously or not, one can only be amazed at how hypnosis facilitates a trait that in waking life Ray Bryant has no talent for.

His most significant recollection is of the life and times of a man called Reuben Stafford. Stafford was born in Brighton (or Brighthelmstone as he correctly identifies it at the time) in 1827. He moved to Lancashire, serving as an ordinary soldier in a regiment based in Preston. His first past-life memory was of the bandstand he enjoyed at Fulwood barracks. He went on to serve in the Crimean War and suffered a minor injury in the hand, while attacking a quarry near Sebastopol in 1855. While he was recovering he was tended by 'Florrie's Ladies', as he termed the nurses led by Florence Nightingale, who did indeed serve in the Crimea. On his return to England, Stafford became a sergeant at Fulwood barracks until moving to London to be near his son, who was an articled clerk. But in 1879, depressed and lonely, he killed himself by jumping into the docks at Millwall.

The siege of Sebastopol in 1855. Was this the dramatic scene of Ray Bryant's past-life?

Ray Bryant has been able to describe this life in great detail. At first it seemed as if these recollections would never be verified, but after much effort some obscure military records were traced to prove that the soldier Reuben Stafford had really lived and that the story told about him by Ray Bryant was accurate. Researchers tried to trick Bryant by leading him into false claims. They had a record of the life and times of his regiment and barracks but had shown none of this to Ray. He was not caught out, and only related details that fitted in with the facts already known. There had even been a bandstand exactly where Ray, as Stafford, had described seeing it at Fulwood, even though it had been pulled down many years before.

Eventually, and without telling Ray Bryant of the discovery, the death certificate of Reuben Stafford was traced. It matched perfectly the details that were told under hypnosis by a man who was born 60 years after Stafford had committed suicide.

Researchers tried to trick Bryant by leading him into false claims. They had a record of the life and times of his regiment and barracks but had shown none of this to Ray. He was not caught out, and only related details that fitted in with the facts already known.

Of course, all the problems of cryptomnesia recur here. Since the records which were eventually found matched with Stafford's life and death, details of his regiment, barracks and war service, it could be said that Ray Bryant had access to them. Indeed, he may have come upon them at some point during his life, even if he did not consciously remember doing so. Yet these details were located in various obscure sources and no single easily obtainable record has yet been traced that contained them all. Indeed, if this was cryptomnesia, what made Ray Bryant want to fantasise this life of a man who was just an ordinary soldier and who lived a short and very mundane life in Victorian England?

Master of Past Lives: The Psychologist's Investigations

THERE IS LITTLE QUESTION as to which scientist has done the most to investigate reports of alleged past lives in a serious way. This has to be Professor Ian Stevenson, a psychiatrist from the University of Virginia. For over 40 years he has produced a mountain of research papers on the subject. These papers exhaustively document evidence that he cautiously terms 'suggestive' proof of reincarnation.

Stevenson has little faith in regression hypnosis, because this is known to produce fantasy as well as memory. But he has investigated many cases of alleged past-life memories that come from spontaneous recall.

This is particularly true in nations such as India, Sri Lanka or Thailand where reincarnation is an accepted religious doctrine, as in many major world religions. Because of this acceptance, when a young child talks about a memory of a previous existence the details are recorded, rather than suppressed by the family, as would be the case with any western culture.

Stevenson has investigated hundreds of reports from Asia, and a few from elsewhere. A typical example involved a young boy who recalled a previous life in a nearby village where he was murdered. The details were then passed on to the police in the hope that they might arrest the person responsible for the recent, and still unsolved, death of this individual. That did not happen but the child conveyed information that seemed to suggest he really had been the man who was murdered shortly before his birth.

A number of difficulties arise from Stevenson's work. In nearly all cases the child recalls a life within a few miles of his current home, certainly in the same country, and often one that ended very recently with many relatives still alive. A study by sceptic Ian Wilson has also shown that surprisingly often the past life was in a higher social caste than that of the present individual. As the countries most often involved tend to have very marked differences between extreme poverty and wealth, Wilson wonders if this rule, that has not been noted in Western past life cases, might indicate the presence of a motive.

By this he means that a poor family could see the advantage of their child claiming to be the dead relative from a recently bereaved and affluent household nearby. They may do so in the hope that financial rewards will be offered by their child's 'previous' family, because their lost loved one has been reborn into less wealthy surroundings. Stevenson counters that there are cases where no such motive is feasible, so it is unlikely that there is widespread fraud.

THE STONE IMAGES · THE STONE IMAGES · THE STONE IMAGES · THE STONE IMAGES · THE STONE · THE STONE IMAGES · THE STONE IMAGES · THE STONE IMAGES · THE STONE IMAGES · THE STONE IMAGES · THE STONE IMAGES · THE STONE IMAGES · THE STONE IMAGES · THE STONE IMAGES · THE STONE IMAGES · THE STONE IMAGES · THE STONE IMAGES · THE STONE IMAGES · THE

CASE STUDY

The Stone Images

MARIA PEREIRA GOT UP as usual on the warm morning of 23 August 1971. It seemed just like any other day, but it was not to be. As she strolled into the kitchen of her small stone house in the Spanish village of Belmez de la Moraleda, she suddenly stopped and just stared. For there set into the concrete floor was a face. Someone seemed to have painted a man's image on her floor. It was definitely not there the day before. But who had painted this picture and why?

Very quickly this 'miracle picture' became the talk of the village and people flocked to the small white building asking to see the image for themselves. Their lives were so disrupted that on 29 August Miguel Pereira, Maria's son, smashed the floor to pieces to destroy the face.

After the kitchen floor was relaid with fresh concrete all seemed well. No new face appeared and people soon lost interest in the Pereira's household. This was until 8 September, when a second face appeared almost in the same place, except this one was even clearer. It was obviously not a trick of the light or a coincidence. The face seemed inset into the floor, and had a stunned-looking expression.

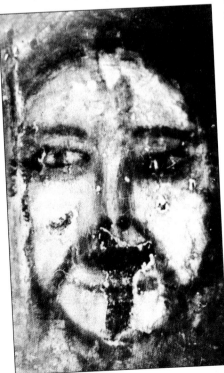

With this new discovery the interest in the Pereira family became acute. Word spread throughout their local area, and each day brought many visitors to disrupt their everyday lives. As the weeks went by the image began to fade, although it did not vanish completely. It appeared to be etched into the chemicals of the floor rather than just laid on top. How it had formed in the first place was still a mystery.

On 2 November, on the orders of the local mayor, the face was carefully cut out of the floor in front of watching crowds and mounted behind glass on the wall by the fireplace. Although much less vivid than when first formed in 1971 it has remained visible ever since.

Immediately after this delicate process was completed the floor was dug out for a second time. This time the workmen went much deeper to reveal the earth under the house. There, quite a distance down, they found the remains of human bones. This immediately led superstitious locals to say that a restless spirit had created the portrait. What was not readily appreciated at the time was that a century before, the entire village had been built on the site of an old graveyard, so the discovery of human bones was unsurprising.

By Christmas 1971 two new faces had appeared on the third concrete floor in the Pereiras' kitchen since the summer. One of these appeared to be that of a woman, but both images appeared to be formed in the same way, either by chemicals or paints printed directly on the floor. By the summer of the following year a number of smaller faces, up to 20 in total, had also started to appear in the kitchen. Each of these gradually faded, and by 1973 the appearance of new faces seem to have come to an end.

But they had not ended completely. In 1983 more faces started to form in the same room and in 1989 the most stunning of all – a life-sized full figure of a man – dominated the small kitchen for a few weeks. The notoriety of the Belmez faces was now assured and, from time to time, images have continued to appear, always very suddenly and without obvious warning.

The question remains: how were these images being created, and why?

One of the legendary 'Belmez faces', which appeared from 1971 to 1989, confounding any conclusive attempt at scientific verification.

Painted Images:
The Scientific Studies

THE FIRST PEOPLE TO EXAMINE the Belmez paintings were artists. Fernando Calderon saw the first ones in 1971 and considered them to be masterpieces in the expressionist style. He thought that it was unlikely that the inartistic Pereira family could have done them.

This was totally disproved on 9 April 1972 when a visiting professor of parapsychology, German de Argumosa, observed with several other people a painting forming on the floor. There were initially just a few lines, but over the course of several hours a face emerged. Several photos were taken as the face evolved, but it did not last beyond that day.

This event then attracted the interest of Professor Hans Bender, one of the first full-time paranormal researchers in Europe, who ran a department at the University of Freiburg in Germany. Bender was intrigued because the portraits were interpreted in different ways, depending on the witness. They all saw a face, but some said the image was of an old person, while others thought it was a youth.

To his credit Bender tried hard to unravel the mystery. He carefully laid some plastic sheeting over the entire floor and attached it to the wall in such a way that it could not be easily removed. He wanted to set up cameras to automatically film the kitchen and the creation of the faces, but the very dim lighting in the small room made this impossible. He had to keep returning to check out the floor. Unfortunately, condensation formed under the sheeting and obscured the view before any images appeared.

Ghost investigator Andrew MacKenzie visited from Britain some years later and made a very careful study of the second wave of faces. The case was now considered of prime significance by the paranormal research community.

> *The portraits were interpreted in different ways, depending on the witness. They all saw a face, but some said the image was of an old person, while others thought it was a youth.*

The most important recent investigation was conducted by Spanish researchers Cesar Tort and Luis Ruiz-Noguez. The significance of their work is that in 1993 they were able to report on modern chemical analyses made on one of the faces. No obvious paints or pigments were found, suggesting, but not conclusively proving, that somebody was not merely painting the images as sceptics had very reasonably contended. Moreover, as had been found with the earlier faces when Dr Bender was involved, they were not easily removable by scrubbing or using bleach. They did indeed appear to form out of the chemicals within the floor itself, although by what process was far from clear.

In the end Tort and Ruiz-Noguez speculated on the possibility that some psychic process was manipulating the atoms of chemicals in the floor so that the pictures could be formed. This could be similar to the way chemical developers allow a photographic image to appear from a film. But they also noted that such speculation would be very difficult to confirm and that tests should continue to absolutely eliminate any possibility of fraud.

More Strange Faces:
Other Reported Findings

ALTHOUGH THE BELMEZ FACES are certainly the longest-lasting and most extraordinary of such phenomena they are by no means unique. In 1923 an image appeared on a wall in Christ Church, Oxford. What seemed to be a face formed on the damp patches of a wall and remained for some weeks, attracting much attention. The resemblance was uncannily like that of Dean Liddell who had served the church, but had died in 1898.

The image bore such a strong resemblance to Dean Liddell's face that it seemed likely that someone had drawn it. But as no evidence was ever discovered to prove that, it was felt that it could have been made by some supernatural process. The connection between an image and the fact that it was found in a church appears to be a very important factor.

However, an incident that occurred at the Same Yet Inn in Prestwich, near Bury in Lancashire, in March 1994, is even more mysterious. The inn had a reputation for

Dean Liddell (left) who served at Christ Church, Oxford until he died in 1898, and (right) the image that appeared at the same church in 1923 – a quarter of a century after his death.

strange phenomena. There had been reports of unusual noises and bottles that moved without anybody touching them. Then one day the image, or shadow, of an elderly man appeared to form on one wall.

At first glance this might well have been considered to be the human mind reading the shape as a face, which had probably formed on the wall through natural processes such as damp. However, the other strange phenomena were attributed, as was the belief that was prevalent among a few locals that the spirit of a farmer, killed on the site in a robbery 150 years before, might have been to blame.

As these matters were being considered, disaster struck. A terrible fire ravaged the building in the middle of the night. There was considerable damage, but the fire brigade were puzzled as to exactly how it had happened, and why very little residual heat was left behind.

One wall in the building survived without damage. It was the wall on which the shadowy image of the old man had been previously found.

The Synchronicity Theory: A Psychologist's View

CARL JUNG, THE FAMOUS Swiss-born psychologist was probably the father of modern-day paranormal research. Although he never viewed himself as anything other than a doctor and researcher who treated his patients to help them recover from illnesses and phobias, he had an abiding passion for mysteries of the mind.

In his many published works spanning the late 19th and first half of the 20th centuries, Jung often described such well-recognized modern mysteries as out-of-body states, precognitions and clairvoyant visions. He was not one to dismiss them as unimportant. Indeed, many of his views about the way the mind functioned were based at least partly upon his observations of such phenomena. He lived long enough to publish what is even today regarded as a very perceptive book on UFOs, just before his death in 1959.

One of the main theories formulated by Jung was the idea of the collective unconscious. He believed that all of us have a conscious, thinking mind, and also a deeply unconscious one which stores images and powerful motifs carried from generation to generation. He believed that this unconscious imagery surfaces in altered states of awareness, such as dreams or hypnosis, making them useful to help diagnose deep-rooted problems. However, he also felt they were a useful way to access potentially super-normal information. Jung argued that, beyond the individual unconscious, there was a kind of super-mind where the collective driving forces and images of our entire race were linked in some way. He likened our individual minds to atolls growing out of a huge all-surrounding ocean.

When physicists began to discover the inner basis of matter, and how atoms were a seething mass of energy fields, Jung saw the potential to explain some of the riddles of human experience. He was particularly interested in what he had come to regard as meaningful coincidences, not just random events, but what appeared to be amazing incidents that worked to an individual's advantage. To him the mind was able to somehow manipulate these things into taking place, possibly at such a level where the unconscious mind of an individual, the collective unconscious of all people and the energy fields controlling the functions of all matter might be made to work together.

Along with the renowned physicist Dr Wolfgang Pauli, Jung set out what he called the theory of synchronicity. This explained how seemingly random events might, in fact, be linked below the surface, and result from some order and pattern of which we were normally unaware of being imposed on our existence.

> *Jung believed that all of us have a conscious, thinking mind, and also a deeply unconscious one where images and powerful motifs carried over the generations are stored.*

Nothing that has emerged from the fields of physical science and paranormal research in the 50 years since that theory has demolished the possibility. Indeed, in many ways, the value of the concept has been strengthened and may offer the best way to understand seemingly very peculiar phenomena such as the Belmez paintings.

'Thoughtography': Images Created by the Mind

ONE OF THE WAYS IN which the ideas of Jung may be seen in action is a rarely reported phenomenon known as 'thoughtography'. If Jung's theory is right it may happen much more often at an unconscious level. American bell-hop Ted Serios found many such anomalies appearing on photographs that he took. These were dark lines and white spots and occasionally fuzzy images of things that were not there when he took the picture. He could not understand why they kept forming on what should have been routine photographs.

During the 1960s Serios spent years working with Dr Jule Eisenbud, a professor of psychiatry at the University of Colorado, to try to create images on undeveloped film placed inside various cameras. He attempted to do this simply by thinking of an object. The process was carefully checked for fraud, but it was never proved and some of the things that Serios apparently 'imaged' inside his camera were different from how they should have appeared in reality. Buildings that did exist had incorrect spellings on their hoardings, or pictures of museum exhibits were similar to the original display but slightly different. It was

as if the final image was a combination of a real photograph which became slightly distorted when it was processed through the mind of the 'thoughtographer'.

Since then there have been a number of other studies of people who produce such images. Mostly these happen sporadically and not when the person is subjected to experimentation. So the suspicion of fraud, or that the photographer was just clumsy and the dark patches on their films resulted from their lack of skill with the camera, do inevitably linger.

However, that idea proved very difficult to substantiate with an American woman called Stella Lansing, who was studied throughout the 1970s and 1980s by Florida psychiatrist Dr Berthold Schwarz. Mrs Lansing had numerous psychic experiences in her day-to-day life and produced not only countless still photographs, but several sequences of cine-film that had unexplained items on them. These included human faces that had expressions that were similar to those that formed on the floor in the Belmez kitchen.

In 1992 some extraordinary work was published by Russian psychiatrist Dr Gennady Krokhalev. He experimented with 203 patients at a hospital in Perm. They all suffered from strong visual hallucinations, which occurred as a result of illness or alcoholism. Krokhalev tested them by encasing their heads in a light covering with a camera strapped to their eyes. He got them to describe their hallucinations as they entered into an altered state of consciousness. An amazing 40 per cent of the patients then successfully produced unexplained images on the film that they could not possibly have put there by any obvious means. Often these were just light and dark patches, but some were fuzzy images that did seem to match the hallucinations that they said were also going through their mind at the same time. These included animal horns and the surface of the moon. Alcoholics were seemingly the most adept at this remarkable process.

As a result of this work the Russian research team suggested that thoughtography may be more common than we imagine and that it could be a product of the energy inherent within human consciousness manipulating the sub-atomic energy fields inside the chemicals that make up the film. A very similar process may possibly have been responsible for allowing the paintings to form on the Belmez kitchen floor.

Fairy Images:
The Teenagers' Story

OVER THE YEARS THERE HAVE BEEN many cases of very strange things being seen and even photographed that logically just could not have really been there. One of the most intriguing stories, which was the subject of two Hollywood movies in 1997 and 1998, is that of the Cottingley fairies.

In 1917, ten-year-old Frances Griffiths was staying with the family of her cousin, 16-year-old Elsie Wright, at Cottingley, now a suburb of Bradford but which was then a quiet Yorkshire village. The two girls were fascinated by fairies and claimed they saw them often when playing in a wooded glen with a stream and waterfall just behind the Wright house. Elsie was a good artist and had earned a place at college. She enjoyed drawing fairies, but the girls' families were very unimpressed with their tales from the riverbank, especially as the girls kept falling in while trying to get a closer look.

Determined to prove their stories they borrowed Elsie's father Arthur's camera and returned with what they told their parents was proof that they were indeed seeing fairies. Arthur developed the plate and there was Frances surrounded by dancing winged sprites. Knowing his daughter's skill at drawing fairies, he believed from the start that the picture was just a hoax with Frances surrounded by cutouts of Elsie's fairy drawings. The girls insisted otherwise and produced another picture, this time of Elsie sitting beside a gnome.

Two years later the girls' photographs found their way to a spiritual association thanks to Mrs Wright. From here the rather unconvincing images reached famous novelist,

PHOTO W. RANSFORD
LONDON N.W.

Sir Arthur Conan Doyle, the famous novelist who propogated the Cottingley fairy myth.

Sir Arthur Conan Doyle, who was by now deeply interested in the paranormal and also writing an article about real-life fairy sightings.

He then persuaded the girls to take more photographs and they came up with three further shots in 1920. They then moved apart and the story was left to Doyle (who went on lecture tours and wrote a book) and other believers to ensure that the legend lived on.

In 1971, a now elderly Elsie appeared on BBC TV and five years later was reunited with Frances at Cottingley for a final TV appearance before their deaths. They stuck by their story, but they did add a few enigmatic comments, suggesting that the fairies were real but the photographs were of their imagination. At the same time computer enhancement techniques for studying the photographs revealed strong evidence that they were not real but two-dimensional, cut-out drawings just as Arthur Wright had suspected on the day the very first plate had been taken. You could even see the hat pin used to hold up the gnome.

Following this work paranormal researcher Joe Cooper, who had collected many modern-day stories of fairy sightings, finally got the women to admit the hoax. They would have confessed sooner, they said, but the momentum was so great that it was difficult to stop, particularly after Doyle took on the role of their champion.

However, to her dying day Frances insisted that they really had seen fairies and that, while they faked the first four pictures, the last one was real. They had seen something in their minds and this had somehow appeared on the photographic plate. Elsie Wright however, remained silent at her friend's statement. But is it possible that their fervent desire to prove themselves and show that the fairies were real was enough to allow a thoughtography experience to happen?

The Man on the Marsh: The Templetons' Story

A MODERN-DAY COTTINGLEY PHOTOGRAPH was taken on a fine Sunday in May 1964 by Carlisle man Jim Templeton. I am satisfied that the story is not a hoax, as he and his family remain adamant it is not. His daughter Elizabeth had a new dress and the family set off for Burgh Marsh, a pleasant spot near the Solway Firth. The plan was to take some photographs of the girl in her new outfit. Jim recalls how, as he used his Pentacon camera to take a number of shots, the weather seemed rather strange. The air was heavy and there was an electrical feel to the atmosphere as if a storm was about to break, although in fact the day remained fine. In addition some cows in the field were also behaving rather oddly, as if they were affected by the conditions.

The Templetons had a pleasant afternoon and saw almost nobody else on this fairly isolated and sometimes dangerously tidal spot before they made for home. But when the colour prints were later developed from their camera, the family received a disturbing and stunning surprise. What should have been the best shot of little Elizabeth holding a bunch of sea-pinks was ruined by what seemed to be a man in a spacesuit standing behind her.

The Templetons thought this was very strange as there had been nobody standing there. Jim could not have missed someone in a spacesuit standing right next to his daughter, and his wife saw nothing and she had been nearby watching the picture being taken. Yet suddenly there was this strange man in their photograph.

In fact, you could see the upper half of the body which was wearing a white suit and a face through a transparent visor. The rest of the body was out of sight behind Elizabeth. Also, if you worked out where the legs should be, the person would not have been standing on the ground but floating at a slightly odd angle. This is a feature often found in photographs produced by thoughtography.

To this day nobody knows what is on that photograph. I visited the Templetons, who still live in Carlisle, 32 years after the picture was taken, and saw the original print and camera as well as a huge enlargement. There

> *What should have been the best shot of little Elizabeth holding a bunch of sea pinks was ruined by what seemed to be a man in a spacesuit standing behind her.*

seems little doubt this is not a film fault or processing mark. The better the definition, the more obvious it becomes that there really is a man in shot – but it is a man who simply was not there at the time. Kodak, the film manufacturer, eliminated the likelihood of a double exposure where one shot is accidentally overlaid onto another. They were so baffled, in fact, that they offered a prize to any employee who could solve the riddle. Nobody claimed it. The police also investigated the matter, and even brought in the help of the forensic laboratories. After weeks of study they merely concluded that it was 'some sort of freak picture'.

If this image was somehow imprinted onto the film by a person's mind then there are interesting reasons why it took the form that it did. Jim Templeton was a fireman and the resistant suits sometimes worn by such crews are similar to that of the man in the picture. Space travel was new and exciting and very much in the news in 1964 and so was bound to be very much in the public consciousness. There was even a nearby plant that assembled Blue Streak missiles which were being launched from Woomera in Australia as part of what was an abortive British attempt to enter the space-race. And a short distance across the marsh from where the image was taken was a nuclear plant where similar protective suits were worn, although nobody was working there on that particular day. So perhaps the image on this photograph was appropriate after all.

Simulacra: The Findings

B OB RICKARD IS EDITOR of *The Fortean Times*, a magazine that gathers strange stories from around the world. He explains that a simulacra is an image with a remarkable visual similarity to something else, that appears either on a photograph or in the world at large.

The Fortean Times has a regular page devoted to pictures of these things, which can be many and varied. There are numerous trees and rock formations that appear in the guise of a human face or body. There are odder events such as clouds floating over Thai temples that resemble sacred elephants. Of course, as Rickard acknowledges, most of these are not paranormal. Fortean events are merely strange and fascinating. They do not need to be supernatural. Often these effects occur simply as a result of the richness of nature and the millions of possible shapes and patterns, some of which are bound to look like recognizable artefacts purely through statistical circumstance.

Many photographs submitted to paranormal researchers result from this effect. I have been shown many examples by witnesses convinced of elves hiding in a tree, for example, which were not seen when the photograph was taken but became obvious after the print was developed. To my eyes it is clear that the effect of light, shade, sunlight and leaves has created an impression that works on the mind. Human beings love to see order in random chaos. That is why ancient man created shapes from the stars and the mythology of constellations such as 'Orion the Hunter' came to life.

The same process is used extensively by psychologists who show patients a random pattern created by ink blotted onto paper and then ask them to describe what they think it looks like. Most people will create an order into this pattern and see it as a rabbit, or a clown, or something different. How their mind transforms the image can tell the doctor important things about the way the patient's mind works.

On other occasions there is a real phenomenon present, but its form is viewed as being more structured. In one case a series of photographs of a 'miracle' in the sky were taken in Rhyl, Wales. The witnesses who took them saw the phenomenon as some kind of angelic vision, likening it to the famous vision of the Virgin Mary seen by many at Fatima in Portugal in 1917. In truth, as the pictures reveal, this Welsh miracle was unusual-looking, but nonetheless just a natural effect caused by the sun shining through ice crystals in the atmosphere.

In December 1996 one of the most extraordinary simulacras brought traffic to a standstill in the centre of Clearwater, Florida. People stood and stared at the magnificent glass-fronted Seminole Finance Building where a gigantic rainbow-hued image of what they took to be the Virgin Mary had appeared. It lasted for some weeks and in the run-up to Christmas crowds gathered, some even kneeling in prayer before the rainbow.

The explanation was that water sprayed from sprinkler machines had settled on the vast panes of tinted glass. This created multi-coloured reflections as the sun shone through the frontage like a prism. While this may have been scientifically accurate, to the thousands of people who saw this spectacle as a sign from God it was the emotive image itself and not how it was created that held importance.

Faces on Mars: Viking's Pictures

UNDOUBTEDLY, THE MOST fascinating simulacra was discovered in July 1976. It was not in the most obvious place to seek out such an anomalous image. This one appeared in two separate photographs taken by the NASA space vehicle, Viking, as it circled the planet Mars.

When the 'face on Mars' was discovered in a picture from the Cydonia region, NASA was quick to refute it. It certainly appeared very convincing as it was about a mile across with a full facial form including hairline, eyes and nose. There was no question that the pattern was real. It also appeared rather significant that the image was invisible to any telescope on Earth. You had to be in a spacecraft orbiting Mars in order to see it.

But NASA argued that it was nothing more than a simulacra, created by the effects of light and shade reflecting off mountains and craters that cover the planet's surface. A number of scientists working on the Mars Mission project disagreed. Dr Brian O'Leary, a physicist and astronaut who trained to fly to Mars on a flight that was later abandoned soon after the Viking surveys, showed me the very detailed images that were sent back from the Cydonia region. These pictures make the image of the face appear even more impressive. As far as he was concerned there was good reason to suspect that this was a genuine artefact, that was similar in form to the Sphinx on Earth. As no humans had ever been to

Human beings love to see order in random chaos. That is why ancient man created shapes from the stars and the mythology of constellations such as 'Orion the Hunter' came to life

Simulacra or 'Sphinx'? The 'face on Mars' taken by NASA on the Viking mission of 1976.

surface. Fine details such as eyes have even been brought out in this way.

A 'Mars Mission' project was created in April 1998 to press NASA to take more detailed photographs using more up-to-date technology. These, it was hoped, would prove what the researchers already believed – that aliens once lived on the red planet.

Mars this meant that if it was a constructed object then alien visitors must have forged it in this shape.

Over the years a number of detailed studies on the photographs of the face have been made by computer experts. These have led to the creation of a computer mapped three-dimensional model. From this it appears as if there really might be a constructed object on the

Unfortunately, the study, when it was carried out, apparently demonstrated just the opposite. NASA was right all along and the face is just the most extraordinary coincidence. It seems that people saw what they wanted to see: the huge 'face' was, in reality, in what was nothing more than a random series of shadows formed by natural rock formations.

SO WHAT DID HAPPEN?

The faces that appeared on the kitchen floor in that small Spanish village are real enough. But how do they form? You have seen the evidence. Now try to decide what the answer might be.

● *Could they be a hoax? Have the Pereiras themselves somehow produced them in order to gain publicity? If so, then why did they destroy the first one so quickly and appear loath to attract more visitors to upset their usual routine? If they were faked, and have continued to be faked intermittently for 30 years, then how is the trick done, especially when some have formed in front of witnesses?*

● *Are we dealing with a series of simulacras? Might there be cracks or other chemical features in the floor that allow stains or dampness to*

appear along certain lines, possibly becoming coloured due to the different compounds in the mixture? When these images form in the approximate shape of a human face does imagination take over and allow the viewer to see what they want, or what they expect, to see?

● *Alternatively, could there really be a supernatural phenomenon at work? Could the mind of someone living in the house be creating the patterns in the same way as some people appear able to produce thoughtography? Is their mind somehow interacting with the energy fields that swirl within the atoms of the floor, so that they mould and shape the chemicals in an unconscious fashion? In fact, rather than impressing a photographic image onto a film, they are possibly just forcing their artistic talents onto the kitchen floor without even realizing what they are doing.*

The Playful Spirit

CASE STUDY · THE PLAYFUL SPIRIT · THE PLAYFUL SPIRIT · THE PLAYFUL SPIRIT · THE PLAYFUL SPIRIT · THE PLAY- · THE PLAYFUL SPIRIT · THE PLAYFUL SPIRIT · THE PLAYFUL SPIRIT · THE PLAYFUL SPIRIT · THE PLAYFUL SPIRIT · THE PLAYFUL SPIRIT · THE PLAYFUL SPIRIT · THE PLAY- · THE PLAYFUL SPIRIT · THE PLAYFUL SPIRIT · THE PLAYFUL SPIRIT · THE PLAYFUL SPIRIT · THE PLAYFUL SPIRIT · THE PLAYFUL SPIRIT · THE PLAY-

THE DAY-TIME HEAT WAS oppressive as August 1977 neared its end. Peggy Hodgeson was struggling to bring up her family of two boys and two girls after the break-up of her marriage. The eldest girl, Margaret, was revising for exams as she prepared to start back to school after the summer break. The younger children felt restless with the stifling weather. Their three-bedroom, semi-detached house in Enfield, Middlesex seemed very small and confining at times. After coping with her children, Peggy simply wanted some personal peace and quiet after what had been another tiring day.

But that was the last thing she was about to get. From upstairs in the house she could hear loud scraping noises as if the house was being redecorated and all the furniture was being moved. She yelled up to the kids to stop playing about, but they called back that it was not them. Determined to end their mischief Peggy marched into the girl's bedroom. A heavy chest of drawers had been moved some distance away from the wall. Peggy could not work out how it had happened, but decided it must have been Margaret. Janet, her younger daughter, was probably too young to shift it at all. But Margaret was sitting there shaking and saying emphatically that the chest had moved on its own and that she was too frightened to sleep in their bedroom that night.

The family went downstairs but the noises continued. Peggy asked the Nottingham family next door to come round and they suggested mice were living in the skirting boards. This logical theory for the scraping noises was quickly forgotten when a heavy bang came from the wall. 'I think you had better call the police,' Vic Nottingham, a down-to-earth builder stated. 'That sounds like somebody is trying to get in.'

Maurice Grosse, investigator of the Enfield disturbances, with items affected by the entity.

In quick response to the phone call two officers arrived, one of whom was WPC Carolyn Heeps. Seeing that nothing appeared to be wrong, she began to suspect that an overactive imagination had been at work, but detected the sincerity and true fear of the family. WPC Heeps was just about to suggest that they check the loft in case an animal was trapped there when the strange scraping sounds began again. Only this time the noises were coming from across the living room. All eyes turned in that direction. To their astonishment they saw a large wooden chair moving along the floor on its own in a shuffling manner.

Unfortunately, this seemingly paranormal event was just the start of the nightmare. The police left in a hurry after pointing out that no crime had actually been committed so it was not their problem. The Hodgeson family's neighbours had no helpful answer either. Peggy and her four children all refused to spend time alone in their bedrooms, and brought sleeping bags and blankets into the living room so that they could all stay remain together. This was how the Hodgeson family were to spend many weeks, in hiding from the mysterious forces that seemed to have invaded their home.

Eventually, when it was obvious that the noises were not going to stop, the Nottinghams contacted a newspaper and pleaded with them to help the distraught Hodgesons. Reporter Graham Morris arrived from a local newspaper but was reluctant to believe that anything was going on. As he sat in the corner of a room waiting, rather impatiently, for something to move so he could record it with his camera, small household objects started to fly through the air. Before he could react he was hit on the head by a Lego brick that sailed out of the darkness towards him.

Graham Morris was totally confused by the events and sent for help from the Society for Psychical Research in London. They had long experience of dealing with these strange phenomena and, the journalist hoped, might help him to figure out what was happening.

The SPR sent Maurice Grosse, a local man who had recently suffered some odd psychic experiences following a terrible family bereavement. He was soon joined by an experienced London-based paranormal researcher, Guy Lyon Playfair. The two men were intrigued to have an ongoing poltergeist incident to deal with as nearly always the disturbances in these cases had ceased before any researcher reached the location.

Months of bizarre phenomena then followed. The strange occurrences at the Enfield semi lasted much longer than expected. Grosse had believed it would end within a few days, as this is what usually happens in poltergeist cases, but the noises persisted until the autumn of 1978, to become one of the longest poltergeist attacks on record.

By the end of this time Janet, the youngest daughter and the one most severely involved in the events that unfolded, was suffering uncontrolled altered states of consciousness that were similar in some respects to a medical condition known as Tourette's Syndrome. She was admitted to a leading psychiatric hospital for tests and to get her away from the stress of the continued poltergeist attack. But the strange events continued even when she was miles away.

Doctors at the Maudsley Hospital found nothing that was obviously wrong with her. As she grew up she went on to run a nursery and put the awful experiences of her younger years behind her. Nowadays, she prefers not to talk about the incidents at all. Margaret, on the other hand, continued to live with her mother Peggy in the same house for 20 years. Over this time she has gradually been able to talk about the odd occurrences. The strange period had a profound effect on the whole family.

Apart from the many moving objects, which included large pieces of furniture such as a heavy sofa literally flying through the air at one point, there were other regular phenomena. As they continued, the two girls claimed that they were even sometimes levitated out of their beds. This was witnessed by several people, including Peggy and John Burcombe, the girls' uncle, who had come to try to help his family. Then, at the end of 1977 and for a few months afterwards, a voice began to speak through Janet, although it sometimes spoke through Pete, the youngest boy. It even spoke through Peggy when Janet was not living in the house. It was a gruff, male voice that spoke in short bursts and used blunt, slightly rude language. The voice appeared to be coming from the false vocal chords deep in the throat often used by ventriloquists. All those taken over by the voice claimed that someone other than themselves was speaking. This voice said he was an elderly man who 15 years before had died from a haemorrhage. He was buried nearby.

This motion-activated picture caught Margaret Hodgeson being levitated by an unseen force.

Nobody knew what to make of this, but in the same way as the ongoing phenomena the voice gradually began to fade, eventually stopping completely. When it stopped Margaret was 15 and Janet was 13. Both children appeared to have been the focus of the paranormal activity. But could they have been responsible for the voice or were they the catalyst for some spiritual force to make its presence felt? Maurice Grosse, who practically lived with the family for a year, was rapidly won over by the Hodgsons and became convinced that this was indeed a real poltergeist of unexpected ferocity. To him it is one of the most amazing paranormal cases of the 20th century.

EVIDENCE

The Playful Spirit

Strange Happenings: The Psychic Investigation

GROSSE, PLAYFAIR AND MORRIS combined forces to try to resolve this case. Almost as soon as they began their work they were at the centre of really strange happenings. Something truly weird was taking place in the Hodgesons' home.

Grosse recalls how marbles would appear from nowhere and smash onto the floor. Unlike normal objects they did not bounce, but just stuck on the floor. When picked up straight-away they felt hot to the touch. Unfortunately, it was not possible to set up video cameras as these were too expensive to operate at this time, but as the girls slept, Morris placed cameras in the bed-rooms that could be triggered by motion into taking photographs. Because of this system some startling images were recovered.

In one incident they heard a sound like an explosion. Everyone rushed upstairs and the cameras recorded the stunned expression on John Burcombe's face as he discovered a still - sleeping Janet on top of a radiogram 1.8m (6ft) off the ground. Earlier there had been concern for her health as she had suffered what seemed like a violent fit and had run around banging her head against the wall. These attacks were occur-ring regularly at this time. The family doctor was called and confirms that he injected Janet with a large dose of a tranquilizer to make her sleep soundly. So therefore it seems very unlikely that she could have climbed on top of the radi-ogram by herself.

Photographs show both of the girls allegedly levitating from their bed' although the images only really show Janet and Margaret hanging in

mid-air. There is no way to prove that they were placed into that position by supernatural forces rather than by leaping or bouncing off the mattress. However, there was some evidence reported from passers-by that they saw Janet floating above her bed in a pose impossible to reproduce simply by bouncing.

David Robertson, a physicist from Birkbeck College, joined the team to test these incredible stories. His attempts to bounce in a way as to be seen by passers-by from the street below proved impossible by any normal means. A distinctive cushion was also found on the roof, seemingly placed there by Janet during one of her floating sessions. Again investigation by Robertson revealed that this could not have been done unless Janet had used a ladder to get onto the roof or, indeed, had floated there by stranger means.

Robertson also attempted to lure the polter-geist into moving heavy objects rather than the small household items it was fond of tossing about. He collected all the objects, such as shoes and toys, and put them out of reach in the middle of the floor. Then a massive ashtray suddenly flew through the air and struck him a nasty blow so he decided not to try to play games with the poltergeist again.

While the team were investigating the voice, many measurements were taken using instru-ments that were hooked up to the girls. These established that if the children were using trick-ery to speak the voice of 'Bill', as the dead man called himself, they were doing so with consid-erable expertise. Years after the incidents had ended the investigators received a letter from a man who said that his uncle had previously owned the Hodgeson house and had died there in the 1960s. This man's birth certificate was recovered in 1995. He was called William (or Bill) Wilkins, and had indeed

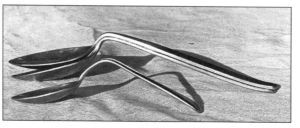

This stone (top) was sliced into three pieces in mid-air, whilst (above) these spoons were warped.

lived in the house. He had died there in June 1963 at the age of 61 from a thrombosis. This was 15 years before his voice spoke through Janet Hodgeson.

The Bull's Head Poltergeist: The Publican's Story

THE EVENTS THAT OCCURRED at the Bull's Head Inn at Swinton in Lancashire would seem very familiar to the Hodgeson family. Scraping noises began soon after the Flint family had taken over the building in January 1985.

The stone pub, originally constructed in the Middle Ages but redeveloped in 1826, stood opposite a graveyard on a road known until recent times as Burying Lane. The unusual scraping noises disturbed Susan Flint as she worked on accounts in a small room near the old cellars late one night. There was very little traffic outside and no customers in the otherwise quiet building. But she was unable to concentrate because of the incessant noises and went to investigate. She was then amazed to see a wooden chair sliding back and forth across the floor.

At first she was convinced that this was just because of traffic and dismissed the matter. But it soon came to light that strange things had happened in the Bull's Head before. These included odd noises and strange voices. The events that happened in this Swinton pub were related to me by some mutual acquaintances. As a result an investigation was mounted by the Northern Anomalies Research Organisation (NARO).

Unfortunately, by the time NARO were involved the activity had ceased, as so often happens. But they were able to eliminate vibrations as the cause of the moving furniture. In addition, there was a terrifying encounter that happened on 8 April, Easter Sunday, which could well have led to a tragedy.

Susan's mother, her stepfather James and a family friend, Andy Cameron, had come around for a visit and late that night Susan broached the

The Bull's Head in Lancashire was the scene of poltergeist activity.

subject of the poltergeist in the pub. Andy was an electronics technician with the RAF and considered the stories to be somewhat amusing. After some debate he was challenged to sleep in the cellar and he and James agreed to face the supposed 'ghost' with brave defiance.

They settled down on stone floor of the cellar and after talking for a time with nothing happening, they zipped up their sleeping bags and fell asleep. Hours later, in the middle of the night, Andy's screams woke up James and both men found themselves staring at some flickering orange lights that glowed in the doorway. Then there was a huge flash of light and the room was suddenly plunged into darkness.

The Flints heard the screaming and came rushing down to the cellar to see what was happening. In the moments before they arrived the two would-be ghost-busters heard the sound of barrels filled with beer crashing into each other. When the Flints put on the lights and stared into the cellar they were faced with two former sceptics who looked terrified. Andy was standing in a corner with a broom that he had grabbed hold of in the dark. He was swinging it wildly, fending off the unseen forces. The noises had stopped and it had gone quiet again.

Andy's screams woke up James and both men found themselves staring at some flickering orange lights that glowed in the doorway.

James was not quite so lucky. He had tried to flee from the room in terror and had crashed against one of the dislodged barrels in the pitch dark. He was lying on the stone floor with blood pouring from a head wound. He needed hospital treatment but the doctors were never told what really happened and James became a changed man after his frightening brush with the supernatural. And Andy, who had thought that the possibility of a ghost was so amusing, would not return to the cellar, even in daylight. The Bull's Head poltergeist had certainly made its mark.

Psychic Temper Tantrums: The Different Theories

THERE ARE TWO MAIN THEORIES adopted by researchers to explain poltergeists and it can be difficult to decide which one is right from the evidence that is reported.

The more exotic idea is that some entity from either the afterlife or another dimension tries to attract attention to itself by extracting energy from the surrounding environment. It then uses this burst of energy in order to 'do' things. This means that a room would go cold, as is often reported during such attacks, because the energy that is needed to move objects is being taken out of the heat energy in the air itself. Since physicists know that you cannot destroy energy, but simply change it from one form into another, there must be some sign of such a transition. It seems possible that this heat energy is transformed into kinetic energy (the energy of motion) and as such the air cools due to energy depletion. Due to the fact that energy has been used to move them, this would account for objects feeling hot after a poltergeist disturbance.

Certainly some poltergeist cases appear to involve entities, like those of Bill and Pete. But are they real spirits, returning to safeguard their mortal haunts or attempting to impart some message? This is unclear as there are cases where a poltergeist has claimed to be a dead person but no evidence for their existence is found.

The other theory is that the attack is the result of a living person who is at the centre of the events. This idea arose when it was realized that poltergeists often attacked houses inhabited by teenagers who were going through the intense physical or emotional changes one experiences during adolescence. Even when no such people were present someone with an emotional trauma of some sort was sometimes at the heart of the incident. This is not true in every poltergeist case, but it has been found often enough for it to appear relevant.

It is sometimes speculated that a sort of psychic temper tantrum may be unleashed by the unconscious mind, and that the person involved is unaware that they are the ones responsible for the seemingly inexplicable events happening around them. The energy that causes objects to move would come from these people, leaving them emotionally drained and physically tired.

Many mediums report that after they have had a psychic experience they need to sleep for hours to recover from the debilitating effects of the experience. Actor Bill Waddington, who served as an entertainer during World War II, told me how he felt that he could act like a 'psychic sponge', soaking out the negative emotions from his battle-weary audience. This process lightened the spirits of the audience, but left Bill himself heavy and depressed as he took on board their low energy. The same kind of energy transfer may occur during a poltergeist attack. There is mounting evidence that there is such a thing as emotional energy and that this energy is critical to the occurrence of paranormal events. This may also be the reason why close family members are often involved in these attacks.

PETE THE PESKY POLTERGEIST: THE PSYCHICAL INVESTIGATIONS

WHEN THE STAFF AT the Cardiff lawn mower-repair company, Mower Services, first heard stones bouncing off their roof and windows they naturally suspected children at play. Yet whenever owner John Matthews ran outside there was never anybody in sight, and the police, who were called out regularly when the bombardment continued for months, failed to come up with any evidence of vandalism. They regularly patrolled the alleyway at the back of the workshop without success.

Then it became clear that the real culprit was a spirit. The half a dozen staff who were subjected to this almost daily assault named this spirit Pete the poltergeist.

In early 1987 a rain of small objects, stones, bolts and even coins began to be thrown around inside the building. Often several witnesses saw that this was happening while nobody was standing in the part of the room from where the missiles originated. In addition, all the staff and several customers, a terrified insurance agent who had come to investigate a burglary was subjected to this regular barrage.

By June 1989, and at the suggestion of the insurers (fearing a claim from a customer who might get injured by 'Pete'), the Society for Psychical Research was asked for help. They sent in Dr David Fontana, a psychologist at the University of Wales. During the next two years he was to witness numerous strange events and conducted a thorough search for rational answers or fraud. He was convinced that the attacks came from a real poltergeist.

Emotional Energy?:
The Physicists' Experiments

THE WORD 'POLTERGEIST' comes from an old German term for 'noisy spirit'. A very significant poltergeist case occurred in the small German town of Rosenheim in October 1967, which led to the first modern scientific experiments into what was taking place.

The siege occurred in a lawyer's office and seemed to be the result of electrical overloads of many different kinds. Light bulbs would explode, the photocopier would go crazy and many fuses would blow without obvious reason. These were accompanied by more typical poltergeist incidents such as rapping sounds that came from within the walls of the building. Filing cabinets were also moved across the room.

One of the most intriguing phenomena concerned enormous phone bills resulting from repeated calls to the speaking clock. No-one in the office was making these calls, despite hundreds of them being recorded each day. It seemed as if there was a fault in the electrical circuits. In many poltergeist cases in the past 30 or 40 years telephone problems, such as unexplained ringing, have become commonplace.

Telephone engineers called to investigate at Rosenheim were unable to explain the problem. They did found power surges, but when the supply was cut and control filters fitted, or an outside emergency power source brought in, the fluctuations were still measured. Something inside the building was responsible for the disturbances but there appeared to be no scientific cause.

By now several physicists from a German university were on the scene trying to understand this baffling problem. They eliminated all obvious sources of energy such as magnetic fields, ultrasonic waves or electrostatic energy charging up the equipment. The telephone involved was monitored all the time. Nobody used it, but still the calls to the speaking clock continued.

Eventually the team realized that the incidents had started soon after a shy 19-year-old woman called Annemarie had begun work at the office and that they only occurred when she was present. She was apparently bored by the work she was doing and used to clock-watch. They suggested that she was somehow unleashing the energy that caused the phenomena and that the calls to the speaking clock were being made unconsciously, presumably by some kind of energy pulse from her mind that was scrambling the electrical circuits within the phone. This allowed her to express her disenchantment with her job in a very obvious and symbolic manner.

After Annemarie was moved to a new job at the suggestion of the investigating scientists, the incidents at the office ceased. But various technical problems with equipment at a bowling alley were still experienced whenever she went playing there with her boyfriend. But once she settled into this new relationship and a more fulfilling job in the spring of 1968 these strange occurrences also died down. Annemarie was no longer at the centre of any poltergeist attacks, which suggested to the researchers that her emotional state was certainly related to the disruption by the poltergeist.

Fontana saw many objects sail through the air when there was nobody around who could have thrown them. Often, when these were picked up immediately, they were very hot to the touch. Pete was also reactive, so if a stone was tossed into an empty corner of the room one would be thrown back. Once, with all the staff standing around a table with their hands in full view of everyone else objects fell from the air on demand. For instance, John said instinctively at one point that they should write down what was happening during this impromptu experiment. He had hardly spoken before a pen followed by a sheet of headed notepaper from a different company in the office above dropped onto the table.

In 1991 there were three sightings by one worker of a small boy sitting on a shelf. He appeared to be dressed in clothing from around the period of World War Two. On the first occasion the vision was only partly formed and had no legs. Later it was more complete and seemed to play with some toys that were in the room. On the last occasion that the child was seen it appeared to wave goodbye.

Soon afterwards the company moved to larger premises and the poltergeist attacks did not travel with them. However, there were some strange noises on the home telephone of the Matthews family and these continued throughout the move. It was as if some electrical energy was interfering with the phone system but engineers were unable to resolve what that was.

All of the reported phenomena from this long-lasting case are common features in other poltergeist attacks. Stone-throwing attacks were first recorded by the Roman scholar Livy in 200 BC. The one thing that poltergeists appear to do with regularity is act like playful spirits.

Psychokinesis:
Experiments with Emotions

THE IDEA THAT SOME KIND of energy burst from the mind can release physical power and move objects apparently without anyone touching them is called *psychokinesis* or PK. There a few people who have been scientifically tested after claiming to be able to move objects in this way almost to order.

One of the most famous of these people is Uri Geller, an Israeli magician, who in 1973 was tested at the Stanford Research Institute in California and baffled physicists there. They found he could start watches that had not worked for years, or stop clocks to order. He then settled in England, and became famous for his alleged ability to bend spoons. This was done as a party trick, since Geller was always a performer first and psychic second. But he claimed to do these things not by magic but by real psychic abilities.

Geller has attracted huge controversy. One of his chief critics has been American magician and psychic sceptic James 'The Amazing' Randi. He has shown that spoons can be bent by deception using well-practised tricks. The two

have had several legal battles but Geller has never been exposed as a fraud. Indeed, he is now a millionaire because of his abilities, he claims, to help big businesses excavate expensive minerals.

Whenever Uri Geller has appeared on television, the relevant stations have had calls from people watching the show who claim that they have experienced PK in their house at the same time. This usually comes in the form of being able to stop watches or being able to make small objects move on their own. Geller suggests that the latent abilities within the minds of many in the audience can sometimes be awoken when he appears. If this is correct, then these sudden bursts of PK might on other occasions be the cause of what appear to be more severe poltergeist attacks.

Tests on some people who have discovered PK skills after Geller's promotion of the subject have been illuminating. Some have moved small targets inside sealed jars, apparently just by concentrating on them. A temperature drop of about 5°C (40°F) as well as a weight loss of several kilograms has been recorded in the bodies of some of those taking part in such tests. Does this suggest that there may indeed be a transfer of physical energy from the person to the object that is moved by seemingly miraculous means?

In 1993 Paul Launds at Nottingham University conducted experiments to see if it was possible for an individual to scramble a computer using unconscious PK. A computer was programmed to randomly run a series of images. In the tests, the subjects were able to make the computer show the most disliked image less often than chance dictated, and vice versa for their favourite image. These early results indicate that emotion may be a factor in triggering PK, and suggests that where emotion and PK are combined these could trigger the major poltergeist attacks.

Philip the Cavalier:
The Researchers' Invention

ONE OF THE MOST REMARKABLE of all paranormal experiments was attempted by a group of researchers in Toronto, Canada between 1972 and 1975. They began their work after seeing a ghost at a local haunted house. They felt that the evidence made most sense if it had been some form of

The power of the mind? Uri Geller, the Israeli-born magician, displaying his psychokinetic powers.

hallucination. But how could several of their group have all seen the phantom at once? They decided to find out whether a ghost could be conjured up by willing it to manifest itself.

What the team did was invent a fictional person – a cavalier called Philip – and invent his entire life history during the English Civil War. For a year they met in a room filled with Civil War memorabilia, sharing anecdotes about their made-up dead man, adding true historical data they had researched, drawing pictures and attempting to make his apparition appear but all this failed.

Then the Toronto group changed tactics. They decided to heighten their emotions by singing songs and holding hands in the way that spiritualists state most readily opens up the channel between this life and the spirit world. After some months of these new experiments the team were hopeful that their phoney phantom would appear.

Instead they were all surprised when poltergeist events erupted in the room whenever they met. Philip never appeared in any visual form but the table used in their work started to levitate then move around the room in sometimes quite dramatic fashion. Light bulbs went on and off, and rapping sounds were heard. These eventually became a code that allowed the team to communicate in simple terms with Philip as if he were real so that he could answer their questions. Philip was the product of their invention, but did not depend upon the opinions of any team member. He acted and responded as if he were a living individual. By working together they had invented Philip but he had become an autonomous entity over which they had no real control.

The group were tested by numerous scientists and found to be quite genuine. One experiment at an American university ensured that all of the team were pushing down on the table and that they could not have lifted it themselves. But when it did levitate as expected, an unexplained upwards thrust measured at 9kg (20lb) was seemingly responsible.

Other groups have since duplicated the methods of the team and there have been further successes. Only one experiment has claimed to have seen an invented ghost. A man who died in London Docklands was invented and his existence promoted to the local community. An apparition of this phantom was indeed seen but it could not have been real because there no such person had ever existed.

So What Did Happen?

You are now in a position to decide for yourself what really did happen in that ordinary suburban house in Middlesex. The poltergeist incidents clearly struck terror into the Hodgeson family, but how did they come about?

● *Was the whole thing a hoax, and perhaps one that got out of hand? Children love to play tricks and they might have first contrived the early happenings in all innocence, only to find themselves having to continue when the adults took the whole thing more seriously than they expected. This seems unlikely because of the obvious problems that were experienced – especially by Janet – the physical evidence that was uncovered and the conviction of the researchers. Certainly nothing in the Enfield case is different from the phenomena reported for centuries during many thousands of poltergeist attacks.*

● *Could there really have been some contact with the spirit a man who died in the same house 15 years earlier? The Hodgesons say that they did not know any of the facts about this man's life and death when the events unfolded and they were not verified until 17 years after they reported the poltergeist attacks. Could the spirit of this man have remained attached to the house and somehow used the children, to communicate with the living?*

● *Or, was this a classic example of a poltergeist that grows out of the product of the combined psychic abilities and mental energies of the people living in the house? Did the objects start to move and strange noises occur because of the unconscious psychic temper tantrums of the teenagers in the family? Did the collective will of all the people who then joined in the 18-month investigation somehow allow the poltergeist to evolve, just like Philip did in that Toronto experiment, becoming an independent entity over which they had no individual control?*

THE TERRIBLE DREAM · THE TERRIBLE DREAM · THE TERRIBLE DREAM · THE
THE TERRIBLE DREAM · THE TERRIBLE DREAM · THE TERRIBLE DREAM · THE TERRI-
THE DREAM · THE TERRIBLE DREAM · THE TERRIBLE DREAM · THE TERRIBLE
DREAM · THE TERRIBLE DREAM · THE TERRIBLE DREAM · THE TERRIBLE
DREAM · THE TERRIBLE DREAM · THE TERRIBLE DREAM · THE
THE DREAM · THE TERRIBLE DREAM · THE TERRIBLE DREAM · THE TERRI-

CASE STUDY

The Terrible Dream

FOR DAVID BOOTH OF CINCINNATI, Ohio the nightmare started on 16 May 1979. It shook him awake with its vivid colours and terrible emotions. It was so realistic that for a few moments he felt as if it were a memory, not just a fantasy.

In the dream the 23-year-old car rental firm manager had seen an aircraft crossing the sky. It was so clear that he could even identify the airline as being 'American' and that the plane had three engines. But it was making a strange sound, and the engine noise seemed too muted to be healthy. Then, as it passed over some fields, the jet seemed to lose an engine, topple over, crash and explode into flames on the ground. The heat was so intense that he could feel it burning his skin as he was awoke gasping into the morning air.

What on earth did this dream mean? He was not intending to fly anywhere and knew nobody booked to do so with American Airlines. Yet this vision had seemed so incredibly strong it was hard to dismiss. But he put it out of his mind, until the next night. Then the dream returned and again he awoke shaking with fear.

By 22 May Booth was so stunned by this recurring nightmare and the unusually sharp images that it contained that he had become certain he was seeing an event that would occur. Never having experienced anything like this before he steeled himself to call the local offices of the Federal Aviation Administration (FAA). The man who took the call made an official log of the report noting such details as the time of day when the crash happened (or would happen) and the logo on the tail fin. But he told the clearly frightened caller that unfortunately he could not ground every American flight indefinitely because of a dream.

David Booth could not escape the awful feeling that he must do something. So, in desperation, he called a flight manager at American Airlines. This man suggested that Booth talk to a dream psychologist. He did that as well, calling the local university for help. Here a dream specialist attempted to persuade him that his images were internal and not a vision of reality. He had nothing to worry about.

On 24 May 1979 David Booth had his dream for the final time. A few hours after he woke up an American Airlines DC-10 jet with three engines developed trouble moments into the flight. Shortly after take-off from Chicago O'Hare Airport one engine was lost and, emitting a strange muted sound, the jet turned on its side and smashed into a field where it exploded into flames. All 279 people on board died. The TV images of the crash scene and a photograph hastily snapped by a passenger on another airline as the plane went down were soon to be imprinted indelibly onto David Booth's mind.

He had seen all this in his dreams for a week. The FAA could only confirm that, as did the stunned airline and university. There was no doubt that David Booth had seen this accident unfold before it happened. He had seen it so precisely that it surely ought to have been possible to stop that plane from taking off and in doing so cheat fate.

Of course, there is no way to know whether the accident was destined to occur and impossible to prevent, or why this man who had no connection to the flight or the doomed people on board should have had this extraordinary glimpse into the future. For the rest of his life David Booth would have to live with that fact.

Chicago O'Hare Airport, 24 May 1979.
Firefighters tackle the blaze of the DC-10
that crashed with the loss of 279 lives.

A Lucky Escape: A Survivor's Story

Actress Lindsay Wagner, star of The Bionic Woman *and* The Two Worlds of Jenny Logan.

HOWEVER, NOT EVERYONE WHO may have been destined to die on that spring day met such a fate. On that Friday, actress Lindsay Wagner was at Chicago O'Hare Airport with her mother patiently waiting to check in to the fated American Airlines flight.

Lindsay was no stranger to the paranormal, although usually as a result of her fictional roles. She had played a psychic in the movie *The Two Worlds of Jennie Logan* and was best known for her TV portrayal in the title role of *The Bionic Woman* in the science fiction series. However, she had also experienced real life 'intuitive' flashes as well, including seeing images of the house that she and her husband would later buy. That was when she was only 14, years before she even met her future spouse.

Consequently, when she started to get a terrible feeling at the airport check-in she listened to her inner voice more carefully than many others might have done. As the time towards boarding ticked away Lindsay could only stare at the unsuspecting faces at the gate, some naturally anxious about flying, but none apparently experiencing what she was sensing. It felt like a wave of blackness was sweeping over her. She could not clarify precisely what it meant, but she knew that it would be very wrong for her to step on that plane. Her mother, perplexed by it all, could see that Lindsay was genuinely distressed and took little persuading to put off the flight. It was relatively simple to take a later flight. With just ten minutes to spare before they would step through the gate without any prospect of turning back the two women decided not to get onto the aircraft and remained instead on the concourse at O'Hare.

As the huge DC-10 rose skyward it is hard to imagine what must have gone through the mind of this actress. She was torn between her inner certainty that some disaster was looming and her doubtlessly fervent hope that it was all just silly imagination. Seconds later, as the jet fell from the sky, giving nobody on board any chance of survival, she knew that her intuition, gut feeling or vision of the future – whatever you would like to call it – had saved the lives of both herself and her mother. But for so many others, young and old, there had been so such reprieve. If only there had been some way to stop them from taking that last flight.

Unfortunately, as David Booth discovered, no matter how certain you are of what is about to occur and regardless of the clarity of your vision of events yet to come, the world will go on as it is meant to go on and seemingly nothing can stop that from happening.

Colliding Fireworks: A Prophetic Dream

DAVID BOOTH IS NOT ALONE in dreaming of the future. Indeed some people do it so often that they have more or less begun a crusade in an attempt to stop the tragedies that they see from ever taking place.

Chris Robinson is one such person. He fights crime and tries to prevent disasters almost as a way of life. He is well known to the Bedfordshire police, his local constabulary, and on many occasions he has passed on remarkable insights. These visions come as ordinary dreams that are often full of symbols. Chris has had so many of these experiences that he has learnt to decode the images and work out what they mean. He writes down all of his dreams and races against time to give the authorities a proper warning. Although he does see trivial things, many of his dreams appear to describe terrible events shortly before they are about to occur.

Some of the symbols he has learned to understand seem odd. When he sees a dog this appears to mean a terrorist (possibly from the image of 'dogs of war' or mercenaries).

THE ALIEN KIDNAP · THE ALIEN KIDNAP · THE ALIEN KIDNAP · THE ALIEN
KIDNAP · THE ALIEN KIDNAP · THE ALIEN KIDNAP · THE ALIEN KIDNAP ·
THE ALIEN KIDNAP · THE ALIEN KIDNAP · THE ALIEN KIDNAP · THE ALIEN
THE ALIEN KIDNAP · THE ALIEN KIDNAP · THE ALIEN KIDNAP · THE ALIEN
KIDNAP · THE ALIEN KIDNAP · THE ALIEN KIDNAP · THE ALIEN KIDNAP ·

CASE STUDY

The Alien Kidnap

THAT AUTUMN DAY IN 1982 began pretty much like any other for Ros Reynolds. But it was to end in a nightmare that would change her life for ever. She was 21 and with her boyfriend, Philip, had set off from East Anglia at about 7pm for a pleasant evening drive on that September night. Their plan was to visit some friends in Corby, Northamptonshire, and they had called ahead to suggest that they would get there a little before 9 pm. It was a taxing drive but the flat countryside made the journey easy and they smiled and chatted as they drove along.

Near Haverhill something odd happened. Strange lights appeared to come out from some overhead power lines almost like lightning. But these disappeared as quickly as they had arrived. However, a few minutes later a blue glow swooped down from the clouds to surround them, hugging their tail as if it were a police patrol flagging them down to stop. But this was no police patrol car. It was an incredible object that had tendrils of energy swirling around it.

As this phenomena had appeared so the engine and lights of their car began to fade. The huge glowing light now stood over a field beside them as if waiting for them to coast to a standstill on what they realized was an unexpectedly deserted road. Where was the traffic? There ought to have been other cars around. But instead they were alone and helpless in the face of this unknown intruder.

In desperation Philip got out and checked the car, keeping an eye on the brooding light that just sat there nearby. From inside the vehicle, Ros noticed that the whole area was in total silence. Not even a bird was singing. The eerie silence that blanketed the countryside was as weird as the UFO that had forced them to a halt.

Nothing seemed to be wrong with the car, but they could not get the engine to start. Then suddenly, like a scene from a horror movie, the headlights simply sprang back to life on their own and the car engine started working once more.

Ros Reynolds. The details of her experience in 1982 only came to light through hypnotherapy.

As the couple looked around they could see that the object was also gone and they needed no persuading to drive away as fast as possible, accelerating along the flat highways with no sign of a pursuing UFO. Ros and Philip shook their heads, still stunned by what had happened, but determined to press on and reach their destination and safety.

However, when they reached Corby their friends' house was in darkness. This was odd as they were at most just a few minutes later than they expected to be as a result of their enforced stop. Nonetheless their banging on the front door brought two startled people to the bedroom window staring down on these visitors in amazement as the couple stood mystified on their doorstep. It was 1am their friends explained. Ros and Philip were four hours late and they had long since presumed that they were not coming.

How could they have lost four hours on that drive from East Anglia? It was just not possible. Yet, impossible or not, the house clock did not lie. It had really happened.

After the trauma of that night the couple drifted apart. Ros, in particular, could not cope with the imposing memories that weighed heavy on her mind. She suffered physically with strange red marks that caused an inflamed sensation around her abdomen. Her menstrual cycle ceased for months. And her head was filled with weird images of grey faces and what appeared to be complex plans for some kind of engine or propulsion system. These came out of nowhere and she could not shut them out. Ros thought she was going mad and locked herself in her room, lost in depression day after day.

It took a long time for her to cope with her life again. Gradually, the young woman was coaxed back to the real world, and she became desperate to understand what happened to her on that night. A new man called Mark came into her life and he suggested that she visit a doctor and be hypnotized to try to remember what took place during the missing four hours. By remembering these things he thought that she might somehow overcome the horrors that had dogged her ever since and make her life normal again.

The hypnosis proved to be a terrible ordeal for Ros; and it was far worse than she had expected. It opened up all kinds of barriers and let images flood out from her subconscious mind, images that appear to have been trapped there and deliberately suppressed. Ros saw herself in a strange room surrounded by little creatures with blue-gray skin and huge dark eyes. They were prodding her with implements and taking samples of her skin and blood. A tall, more human-looking creature stood watching impassively as if supervising what went on.

With these startling memories, Ros attempted to put the jigsaw together and accept what had happened that night. She saw many professionals and doctors who all endeavoured to assist her in this painful process. It took years for her to move gradually forward into a new, self-assured lifestyle. Even so she still cannot escape the fear that one day the creatures might come back for her. And if they do, Ros feels there is nothing that she can do to stop them.

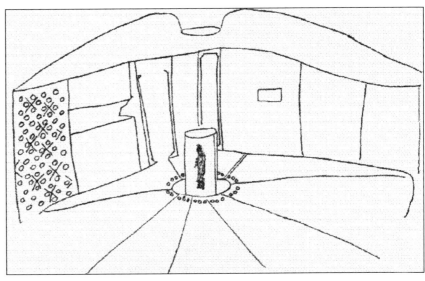

Sketch made by Ros Reynolds of the interior of the space-craft in which she was subjected to disturbing tests by extraterrestrials.

> *They were prodding her with implements and taking samples of her skin and blood. A tall, more human-looking creature stood watching impassively as if supervising what went on.*

ACKNOWLEDGEMENTS & PICTURE CREDITS · ACKNOWLEDGEMENTS & PIC-
TURE CREDITS · ACKNOWLEDGEMENTS & PICTURE CREDITS · ACKNOWL-
EDGEMENTS & PICTURE CREDITS · ACKNOWLEDGEMENTS & PICTURE
CREDITS · ACKNOWLEDGEMENTS & PICTURE CREDITSI · ACKNOW·

Acknowledgements & Picture Credits

AUTHOR'S ACKNOWLEDGEMENTS

I would like to thank the many people who have over the years assisted with some of the cases in this book:

Keith Basterfield, Dr Sue Blackmore, Andy Blunn, Ray Bryant, Albert Budden, Dr Thomas Bullard, Steuart Campbell, George Carpenter, Bill Chalker, Jerry Clark, Loren Coleman, Doris Collins, Paul Fuller, Cynthia and Len Gisby, Maurice Grosse, Dr Keith Hearne, Dr Moyshe Kalman, Joe Keeton, Dr Terence Meaden, Guy Lyon Playfair, Ros Reynolds-Parnham, Bob Rickard, Chris Robinson, Geoff and Pauline Simpson, Jim Templeton, Bill Waddington, Terence Whittaker.

And very special thanks to Peter Hough, with whom I have researched many extraordinary cases for 25 years now. Mulder and Scully have a long way to go to catch up with us!